THE HOME INSPECTION MANUAL
101 Moneysaving Tips to Know Before You Buy a House

ALFRED H. DANIEL

WINGS BOOKS
New York • Avenel, New Jersey

This 1994 edition is published by Wings Books,
distributed by Random House Value Publishing, Inc.,
40 Engelhard Avenue, Avenel, New Jersey 07001,
by arrangement with Storey Communications, Inc., Pownal, Vermont.

Random House
New York • Toronto • London • Sydney • Auckland

Printed and bound in the United States of America

Library of Congress Cataloging-in-Publication Data

Daniel, Alfred H.
    The home inspection manual: 101 things to know before you buy a
house / by Alfred H. Daniel.
        p.   cm.
    Originally published: 1st printing. Pownal, VT : Storey
Communications, © 1987.
    Includes index.
    ISBN 0-517-10116-5
    1. Dwellings--Inspection. 2. House buying. I. Title.
[TH4817.5.D36   1994]
643'.12--dc20   93-48638
                                                                 CIP

8 7 6 5 4 3 2

This book is dedicated to

my spelling expert,

my grammarian,

my editor,

my proofreader,

my friend,

my companion,

my WIFE

and

to all

future home buyers

CONTENTS

Part Three: Covers all *other items,* which
   may or may not be found in and around
   some of today's homes 67

PREFACE

After listening to literally thousands of people complain about the repairs they had to make shortly after moving into a newly purchased home, I began to question the reason for this. Without a single exception the answer was always that not enough attention had been paid to a proper inspection of the house before finalizing its sale. Even people who had purchased several other houses lamented, "All the other houses we bought had problems. We thought from these we knew exactly what to look for, but we certainly got fooled on this one. This house has entirely different problems."

First-time home purchasers, for the most part, are young people without sufficient resources to absorb home repair bills easily so shortly after moving in. What then is the solution? Do purchasers need to hire all kinds of experts to inspect the house to which they may devote a sizeable portion of their income for the next twenty years or so?

A thoroughly experienced house inspector can be of real value to the prospective home buyer. To be worthy of the title one should be widely experienced in the various trades. Simply being an electrician, a plumber, a carpenter, a building contractor, a heating and air conditioning tradesman, or any one or combination of the other trades is inadequate.

Today, more than ever before, construction and the various trades are undergoing great changes which will bring a heavier load to bear on the shoulders of the responsible house inspector of the future. Not only do inspectors need to have the wide experience of yesteryear, but they must also keep abreast of the rapidly advancing technology of today.

Does all this mean the buyer is protected from the unscrupulous or the unknowing? Are the problems being greatly reduced with the employment of these various agencies? Indeed, if this were true, the ever increasing litigations initiated by new purchasers would not be so prevalent.

In meetings with several leaders in the field of real estate and with the head of one state's Consumer Protection Agency, I discussed the need to inform prospective home buyers of the problems that may face them in purchasing a home.

I was so encouraged by all the reports I received that I set about writing an easy-to-read guidebook that would actually instruct buyers in what to look for and not to overlook in making a thorough investigation for themselves prior to their commitment to buy.

Most people cannot afford to spend the $150.00 or so that it costs to have a professional inspection made of every house they are seriously interested in buying. But prospective home buyers can take this book with its checklist and use it successfully on each and every house they are seriously interested in purchasing. When they are ready to take the final step they will be sufficiently informed to be able to make a dollar offer based on facts and costs. In short, they will be intelligent buyers able to make the best deal possible.

It is my intention to open the doors and windows to an area that is shrouded in mystery and eludes most laypersons. Prospective home buyers will be in an enviable position by doing their own house inspection prior to making a dollar offer to buy. The fringe benefits are many: a stronger bargaining position, the proper exercise of the buyer's responsibility, an increase in the pride of ownership, and a savings of hundreds of dollars, if not more.

The accumulation of my many years of experience could be of great help to the prospective home buyer. Showing and explaining where to look is only a part of this book's value. You will also be able to recognize defects and determine their value.

This book was born out of the need to educate the prospective home buyer. You should read it in its entirety before you seriously consider inspecting a house. The information in this book, along with its exhaustive checklist, will turn the home buyer into an informed shopper.

Note: in recent years concerns have arisen about lead, asbestos, ureaformaldehyde, and other building materials suspected of being hazardous to health. It is not this book's intention to analyze such materials. If you have such concerns, by all means seek out and get the best advice available. I recommend the manuals on these subjects that are available from the federal government.

INTRODUCTION

INTRODUCTION

The best help you'll ever find is located at the end of your own arm. This book will help you prove this to yourself.

Who is willing to show the prospective home buyer how to inspect a house? Who will tell him what may be wrong with a house?

Does anyone say, "Why don't you go into the bathroom and look at the tile on the wall around the tub area? Tap on it to see if it is loose?" Does anyone ask you to fill all the sinks with water, remove the stopper, and observe how quickly the water drains out?

Most prospective home buyers will not ask about things that might embarrass the seller. There is an entire range of questions that should be asked, however, without antagonizing the seller or real estate agent, as part of the inspection of a house. Many of these will be introduced to you in this book.

Whether there are problems or not, at least you will have satisfied your mind and personal requirements as a house inspector. Your responsibility is to determine the validity of your findings and their worth. You might equate the inspection you are making to test-driving an automobile.

It is difficult, however, to draw an analogy between purchasing a house and purchasing anything else. This is the largest single transaction many people will make in their lifetime. The purchase price of a house is an investment. Whatever the size of that investment, it is relative to the income of the person making it. Buying a house requires the same determined investigation that one would make before purchasing stocks or bonds.

First the bank demands that the house be appraised to determine its approximate value. Next, by law, an *abstract of title* must be prepared for the property and its *appurtenances* (buildings) to learn if it is free of any and all *encumbrances* and to determine its eligibility for a

3

mortgage. Then a cursory examination is made by the real estate agent to determine its saleability prior to placing it on the market. Finally, some lending institutions, as well as many insurance companies, are now demanding that the house be examined further by a qualified house inspector, prior to their commitments. Each of these steps fulfills an important task in the process of selling a house.

There is a percentage figure for depreciation that is used in the real estate business. When the seller lists his house with a real estate firm, this depreciation factor is discussed, unless the house is new and has never been lived in.

Allowances for depreciation should be assigned to the roof, major appliances, carpeting, etc. Whether there has been an actual reduction in the asking price is a subject for conjecture. Even if a reduction has been made, has it been enough? It is up to you, the buyer, to determine this. Arriving at the *true* worth of the house is your responsibility, in which this book will assist you.

The house inspector should make a written report as to the findings. The inspector will *not* warrant that anything that has been inspected is free of defects. Based upon the findings, an opinion will be rendered as to the apparent condition of the house and of everything that is part of the real estate in question.

There are some preliminary steps you should take before inspecting the house of your choice. First, call the real estate agent (or the seller if the house is being sold by the owner without the assistance of a real estate agent), and make a daytime appointment to revisit the house. Explain that you wish to inspect the house personally before making an effort to buy.

Now get into older clothes. Depending upon the type of house it is, you may be climbing into the attic or onto the roof, squeezing through the access door into a crawl space, and generally getting a little dirty. It will be worth the effort.

Next arm yourself with a reliable pen, a steel tape measure, a screwdriver (with both Phillips drive and blade drive), a flashlight, a pair of cotton gloves, an inexpensive respirator, a pair of binoculars, and the checklist in the back of this book. If you wish to go into the attic you will need a stepladder, and you will need an extension ladder if you are going on the roof. You are now ready to proceed with your house inspection.

Happy reading and house hunting, INSPECTOR!

PART ONE
INSIDE

1 · INSIDE

Foundation

Every house has a **foundation** (base) on which its walls rest. The foundation is important to the stability of the entire structure.

It is safe to assume that the outside walls of most houses that are not mobile homes are built on concrete foundations. These foundations, commonly called **footings,** are poured concrete of varying widths, depths, configurations, and density necessary to support the weight above them. (See illustrations #1, #1-A & #1-B.)

The house will be attached to this foundation, whether it is a basement, **crawl space,** or concrete slab construction.

Some apparent problems in the house may be caused not by a defective foundation but by the water pressure or **hydrostatic pressure** in the ground.

The ground of some building sites absorbs more water than others. Unfortunately, not enough consideration is devoted to determining this factor before building a house.

Generally speaking, the higher the **water table,** the greater the hydrostatic pressure. A basement house in a high water-table area is more likely to have moisture problems than if this same type of house were built in a low water-table area.

Conversely, a house with a crawl space may never receive any damage from hydrostatic pressure, because the floor inside the perimeter of the footing is dirt or sand. This dirt or sand allows the water table to rise and fall without restriction.

The concrete slab construction is also free from rising water pressure. The slab is not in the ground but several inches or more above it. This type of construction does not restrict the movement of water.

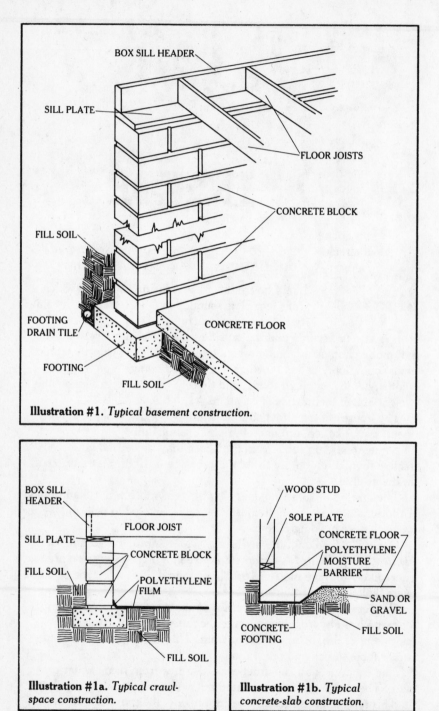

Illustration #1. *Typical basement construction.*

Illustration #1a. *Typical crawl-space construction.*

Illustration #1b. *Typical concrete-slab construction.*

Now that you have the basics (no pun intended) you can approach the house of your choice as any inspector would.

Basement:

You have to start your inspection someplace. Why not the basement?

In most basement houses all of the **mechanicals** (wiring, plumbing, heating, water, and water heater) are located there. In a crawl space or slab construction, however, these same mechanicals are located in a **utility room** and/or under the house. Occasionally these are installed overhead in the attic. Therefore, instead of repeating the mechanicals, they will all be treated in this category.

Did you notice the stairs going down? Did they give you a good feeling of strength and stability? Was there a handrail? Was it firmly secured? And did you have to duck your head going down the stairs? Did you notice whether the light switch was handy? Was it a two-way switch with a corresponding type of switch in the basement? With a **two-way switch** in the basement, you would have the ability to turn on the switch if someone inadvertently turned it off at the other switch while you were down there.

Are the walls painted or paneled? Is the floor painted or is it carpeted? If the basement floor is carpeted and/or the walls paneled, it is safe, in most instances, to accept this as a sure sign of its being moisture free.

Look at the walls and the floor, especially where they join. Discoloration at this juncture is a sure sign of water penetration from the outside. If the walls are painted, the paint may be a waterproof type that indicates a possible past water problem.

Should you notice any of these "dead giveaways," stop here and ask about the water damage or seepages. If you ask a direct question, hopefully the person asked will give you an honest answer. They may truly not know the answer, which is cause to look more closely as you proceed. At least make a note of what is apparent to you.

Basement Windows:

Basement windows can leak a lot of cold air in the winter. If they are steel, they'll probably be painted, rusty, or both. Aluminum windows will look the color of bare aluminum metal. Metal transmits a greater amount of cold than wood. It is important in this day of increasing utility costs to reduce this air leakage problem to a minimum.

Look at every one of the basement windows. Are they covered on the outside with storm windows? Do any have cracked glass in the windows or storm panels? If these windows do not have storm panels and you wish to consider this as a "must include" item, you can determine the cost of each to be about the same as the cost of regular-size house storm windows.

In addition to leaking cold air in either direction, basement windows can also have a problem with moisture seepage if they are at or below **grade level**. If they are below grade level, each of these windows will have a **window well** installed on the outside. Ideally, these wells should be filled with 12–15″ of sand or gravel, beginning several inches below the basement windows, to enhance drainage. You can check this when you are on the outside. If these wells are filled with soil, it will compact and on certain occasions cause the windows to leak water. When the ground is saturated from fall or spring rains and a large amount of water is added by a heavy downpour, the outcome is obvious. The wells fill to overflow and seep in through the windows.

As an aside, a plastic bubble (as shown in illustration #2) is being manufactured in a configuration to fit over both the window and the window well. This **window well cover** is transparent and, if properly installed, waterproof. In addition, it provides some insulation.

Floor Drain:

You will now want to examine the floor drain. A **deep-seal floor drain** (as shown in illustration #3) should have a float ball in it that is active when water is poured into the drain pit. Remove the perforated lid if you can easily do so. With your index figure, push the float ball down into the water. It should rise and reseat itself against the rubber gasket on the bottom of the brass fitting immediately after you release it. Sometimes a float ball has been damaged and is not present. No float ball means you have no protection against sewage water back-up.

This drain is connected to the sanitary sewer line outside the house. It is used when there is no sump pump involved and the floor of the basement is considerably above the street level. It is absolutely essential that it function properly.

If you prefer not to put your finger in the floor drain, fill a pail with about two gallons of water and pour the water into the drain. It would be a good idea to do this anyway to see if the drain is sluggish and how it reacts to the force of water. Many times the washing machine empties into this drain and deposits lint on the drain lid. The lid is perforated and needs to be cleaned periodically. And dried lint at the

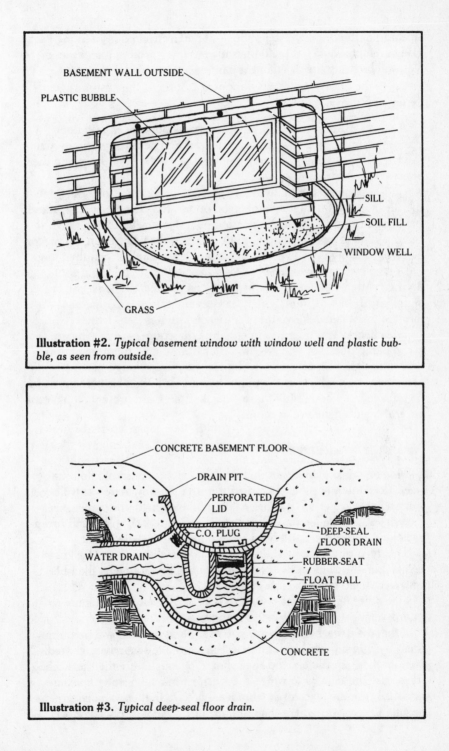

Illustration #2. *Typical basement window with window well and plastic bubble, as seen from outside.*

Illustration #3. *Typical deep-seal floor drain.*

opening of the drain will keep the float ball from properly seating itself. (Be careful to keep lint build-up removed from around the gasket if you will be using the drain in the same way.)

Sump Pump:

A **sump pump** must be present if there is not a deep-seal floor drain. A sump pump is a mighty powerful and necessary part in maintaining a dry basement. Its function duplicates the floor drain and then some. (See illustration #4.)

Go to the pump and activate it yourself. Just lift the rod going down into the sump pit until it activates the pump. Release the lift rod, stand back, and listen. If the suction action operates quietly that is good. If there is a metal rattling sound in the motor while it is running, a **motor bearing** is likely defective. That is a problem signal. When the pump has completed emptying the excess water in the pit, it should shut itself off. Water that is in the discharge pipe will drain back into the sump pit. If there is more water than several quarts draining backward into the pit, it is indicative that the **check valve** is defective.

The check valve operates in only one direction — out. When a sump pump does not remove the water from the pit but only churns the water, this indicates that the bottom of the discharge pipe near the connection at the base of the pump has a hole in it. This pipe needs to be replaced. To correct all these defects, if they are present, could cost several hundred dollars or more.

Washer and Dryer:

Move over to the washer and dryer if they are present. You may need to install a hook-up for yours if it isn't already there. You'll need hot and cold water lines, a drain line, and electricity for the washer. The dryer, if it is electric, will require a separate 220V line and receptacle; if it is gas there will need to be a gas line installed for it.

This type of washer and dryer hook-up installation would add several hundred dollars to the cost of the house if you hired a plumber and electrician to do the job.

One other item you may want to consider in your notes is the cost of a dryer vent. This may add an additional $60 or $70.

If there is a washer hook-up, put your hand on each water line, give them a slight tug, and check to see that they are securely anchored. Neither they nor the electric lines should be loose. Are the **hose bibbs** (these are the faucets to which the washing machine water lines are attached) greatly discolored from leaking? Do they have corrosion around the threads where they are installed? A lot of corrosion will tell

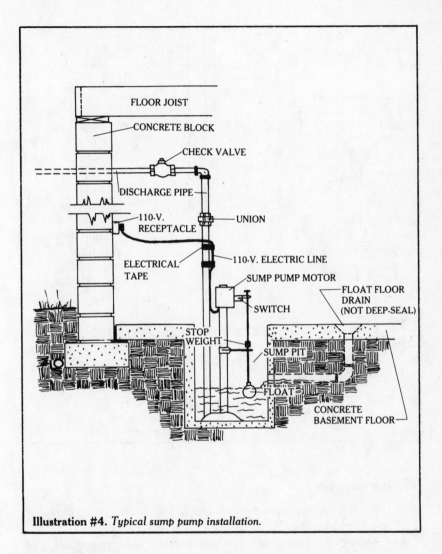

Illustration #4. *Typical sump pump installation.*

you that a problem exists. Replacing hose bibbs is an inexpensive repair job for you to do, and it costs under a hundred dollars to have a plumber replace them for you.

Shower:

If there is a shower in the basement, check it for stability and corrosion. For heaven's sake, turn the shower on! You may learn that it hasn't been used in years and doesn't work well or at all. A basement shower is neither a plus or a minus for the house.

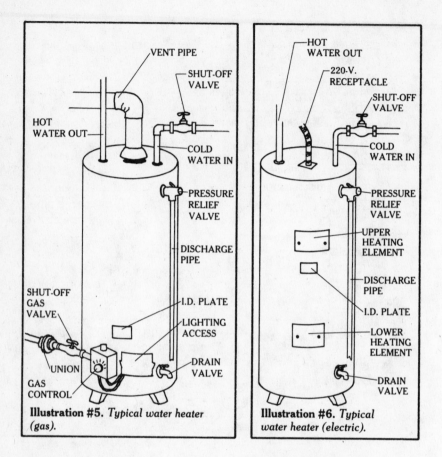

Illustration #5. *Typical water heater (gas).*

Illustration #6. *Typical water heater (electric).*

Water Heater:

It's time to move to the water heater. (See illustration #5.) How old is it? Is it fired by natural gas? What's its capacity for recovery? These are important questions you need to have answered. A 30-gallon natural gas water heater will recover no more than 27 gallons per hour. Somewhere on the face of the water heater near the control will be a metal identification plate. The recovery rate (how many gallons of hot water it will deliver per hour) is printed on this metal plate and shown as G.P.H. (gallons per hour).

Ask the seller when he last drained the water heater. The answer may tell you more about the water heater and its life expectancy than the seller realizes. You'll probably learn that he never has or he can't remember the last time he drained it. In some areas a heavy mineral content in the water can be the cause of a water heater's early demise.

If you want a water heater to last twenty years or longer, drain the water and flush the sediment from the tank at least every two years.

While you are at the water heater, you will want to inspect the **pressure relief valve** to see that it has a discharge pipe. This pipe should run down to within two inches of the floor. If it does not have a discharge pipe, it can be a potential disaster.

If the water heater malfunctions and overheats, pressure builds up in the tank. For this reason it is essential to have a discharge pipe. Instead of the tank's exploding from a pressure build-up, the pressure relief valve activates, releasing the pressure build-up in the form of scalding water and steam. Without a relief valve, a malfunctioning water heater would explode from pressure build-up. A discharge pipe run down near the floor prevents serious injury to anyone standing nearby.

Also notice the in-and-out water lines. Are they very corroded? If so, it's another possible problem. Be sure to make a note of this.

On the top of the gas water heater is an exhaust pipe (usually 3″ in diameter) that carries the gas fumes and heat of operation into the flue. Is the pipe rusted or pitted? Of course, you don't want to punch a hole in it, but if it is very rusty and you touch those spots, they could crumble. What may also alert you to a possibly serious gas fumes leak is tape over or around the pipe. The pipe needs to be changed if it has been taped, since tape does not suffice on pipe with that amount of heat traveling through it.

Ignition burns or blackening on the front of a gas water heater just above the lighting access panel indicates a poor combustion mixture of gas and air. This can occur because of a venting problem or an insufficient amount of air in the gas mixture at the time of combustion. Sometimes this problem is caused by poor ventilation in the flue or insufficient clearance from a wall or storage boxes. (A minimum of 6 inches is sufficient clearance.) It may also indicate that the water heater needs replacement.

If the water heater is electric (see illustration #6), the same questions of size and recovery rate apply. Important to recovery is the wattage size of the heating elements. For your inspection information, 1,000 watts of electricity are required to heat 4 gallons of cold water to a temperature of 100 degrees. Subsequently you have only to multiply the wattage of the elements in the electric water heater to determine how many gallons of water it will heat to 100 degrees per hour. **Normal** operating temperature in most water heaters is between 110 and 120 degrees. **Hot** operating temperature is 140 degrees. Information about the wattage size of the heating elements is located on the identification plate on the front of the water heater.

The electric water heater is silent and gives off no fumes, but sediment occurs just the same as in the gas water heater. Additionally, the lime and iron prevalent in the water begin to cling to the heating elements. Depending on the area in which a house is located, and without the assistance of a water softener, the life span of the heating elements can be greatly reduced, resulting in their needing semi-annual replacement. Make a note if there is not a water softener. Having the elements replaced by a plumber can cost in the $100 range.

Heat recovery of electric water heaters is never as rapid as that of gas. Some areas do not have gas available. This makes electric water heaters necessary where oil or L.P. (liquid petroleum) gas is not permitted.

Water and Sanitary Sewer Line:

Take a few moments to walk around the basement and look up with your flashlight. Do you see wires and water and drainpipes? Of course, if there is ceiling tile or some covering on the ceiling, you'll not see very much.

There are some basement homes in which a portion of the drain and water lines can be seen only by entering through an access door and crawling on your hands and knees, belly, or back. This can be true when the basement is not under the entire house. That portion becomes the same as a crawl-space house. Of course, in a crawl-space house, all of these lines can only be inspected on your back. In some areas of the basement the ceiling isn't covered; that will be around the area of the bottom of the bathtub and toilet. You are looking for several drains — those of the bathtub, shower, toilet, lavatory, and kitchen sink.

The drain that comes out of and is attached to the bottom of the bathtub is called a boot. The boot should have no signs of leakage around it. The same is true of the entire unit called the **trip lever and overflow.** (See illustration #7.)

At the other end of the boot is a tee. Traveling upward from the tee is the overflow pipe. The overflow pipe acts as a safety. Should the tub overfill, the water will empty through this pipe rather than run over the sides of the tub. At the end of the pipe joined to the tub is a large, thick rubber gasket between it and the tub. The gasket should not show signs of leakage. If the boot or the overflow gasket shows signs of leakage, it indicates that a problem has occurred. The drier the appearance of any leak stain, the more confident you can be that there is not a recurring problem.

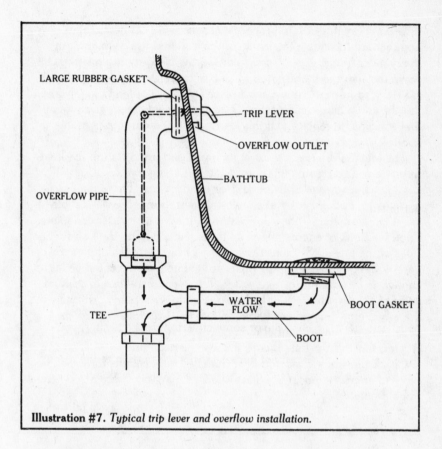

Illustration #7. *Typical trip lever and overflow installation.*

If there is a separate shower, the base of it should be exposed the same way the bottom of the tub is. Again you are inspecting for leaks where the drain connects to the shower receptor. If there are none, move on; otherwise, make a note about it.

There is another kind of leak you should attempt to learn about. The tub (if it has a shower) and a separate shower stall may be the source of leaks only when a person is actually showering. You will not be able to tell if they leak merely by activating the faucets. You would have to actually get *in* to the shower! This will be covered later in the category of the bathroom.

Now locate the drain of the toilet. Your flashlight will reveal stained wood if the toilet has been leaking around its base. You may also see newer support boards between the **floor joists,** which will indicate that there has been a problem and that it may have been solved. It would be well to make a note about this to inspect later when you are in the bathroom upstairs.

Often a lavatory drain proceeds into the wall, connects to an elbow, and then travels down the inside of the wall into the basement. In many older homes (pre-World War II), the lavatory drain travels down through the bathroom floor and is connected to the cast-iron **sanitary sewer** line with a short piece (6″–20″) of lead pipe. Many of the chrome tubings joining these lead pipes break down and require that the pipe be replaced. If this lead pipe is present, make a note about it.

The kitchen drain is similar in its travel pattern to that of the lavatory and will be treated later in the kitchen category.

Check the sewage drains and their connections. These may be partly overhead or partly at shoulder height. Some are 3″ and others are 4″ in diameter. If they are cast iron, they will have leaded joints. Look for signs of encrustations on these joints and on the bottom or sides of the pipes. (See illustration #8.) These rusty-looking encrustations will show up even if the pipes are painted. Some could be large enough to be leaking sewage water. These encrustations are actual holes of varying degrees of leakage. A plumber repairing or replacing these bad pipes may charge several hundreds of dollars or more depending on the amount of damage. If these pipes are plastic or copper, most of the time they will cause no concern.

Check the water lines and their threaded connections for the same types of encrustations. (See illustration #9.) Again, these are potential troublespots.

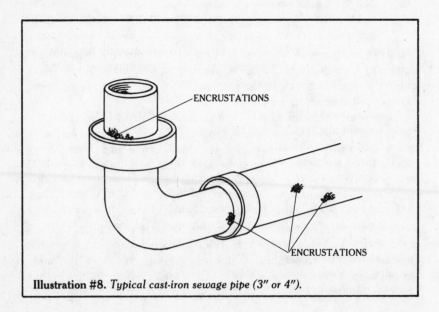

Illustration #8. *Typical cast-iron sewage pipe (3″ or 4″).*

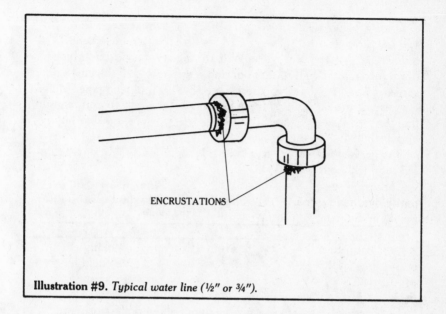

Illustration #9. *Typical water line (½″ or ¾″).*

Main Water Shut-Off Valve:

Sometimes there is paneling surrounding the **main water shut-off valve.** In illustration #10 you will see a typical main shut-off valve. What you see on your inspection may have a different configuration than what is shown in the illustration. That is not important. Regardless of where it is in the basement, be certain to look at it and operate it (if you can). Most valves are operated so infrequently that they become "frozen," requiring a wrench to start the movement of the handle. Don't go to that extent, but do try turning it with your hand.

This valve is very important to the person living in the house. For this reason it will be treated here and again in other categories. This valve should always be easily accessible both for repair and use. In many homes this valve is located in a garage, the front yard, the crawl space, the utility room, a closet, and occasionally in the water meter pit. When these valves are underground outside, (see illustration #11) they can be difficult to operate because the "key" is a ⅜″ steel rod that requires a **locking pliers** or wrench of sorts to activate them. The activation could break the rod. In some homes this valve is broken and inoperable; others are "frozen" and require the water stop valve at the street to be turned off. To operate this type of valve requires the use of a **stop box key.** Even then, many times, these stops are difficult to operate.

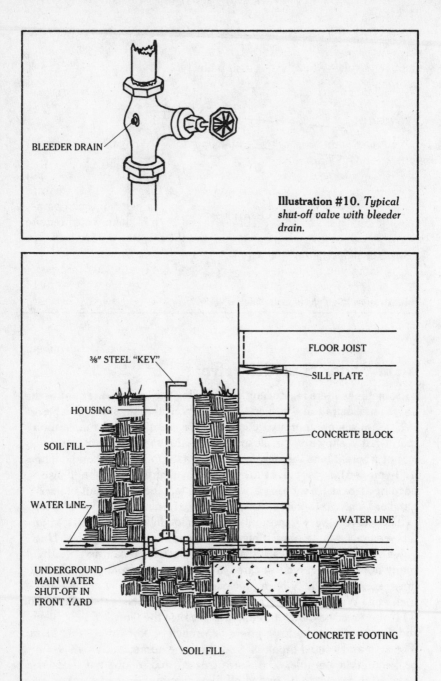

BLEEDER DRAIN

Illustration #10. *Typical shut-off valve with bleeder drain.*

⅜" STEEL "KEY"

HOUSING

SOIL FILL

WATER LINE

UNDERGROUND MAIN WATER SHUT-OFF IN FRONT YARD

SOIL FILL

FLOOR JOIST

SILL PLATE

CONCRETE BLOCK

WATER LINE

CONCRETE FOOTING

Illustration #11. *Typical underground main water shut-off valve installation.*

Be alert to the placement and operation of the main heater shut-off valve. Many homeowners can relate tales about excessive water damage occurring because of their inability to turn off the water in an emergency.

Furnace:

You may want to leave the inspection of the furnace to a qualified heating and cooling firm.

The ways to heat a house vary throughout the country. Houses can be heated by wood; coal; oil; natural gas; kerosene; L.P. gas; steam; hot water; heat pump; electric, radiant, and solar heat; or a combination of these. For you to do your own inspection of them would require taking you through a course in each of these types of heating and cooling facilities.

One thing you definitely want to do is look at the utilities' receipts for the last two years. These will indicate the cost and amount of fuel used to heat the house in the coldest months and cool it in the hottest months. The utilities company will furnish the seller with copies if he no longer has them.

You should be apprised of floor furnaces. They are easily identified by a 30" by 30" (or larger) square steel grill in the floor. They were used immediately following World War II and were installed in smaller, lower-priced houses. These floor furnaces were installed in the center of the house and rarely heated the whole house properly. Floor furnaces can be a danger for a toddler or the disabled because the traffic pattern makes it difficult to avoid walking on them. For this reason floor furnaces are no longer used in residential construction. They are still manufactured and used as replacement furnaces. They also are difficult to work on because you must get under the house to service them.

When you find a house with a floor furnace as its source of heat, it would be well to make a note that you will want to change it to a less dangerous and more efficient type of heating system.

Wiring:

It may be a small point now but begin to count attached light fixtures (where you will be furnishing light bulbs). Continue counting them as you go through the entire house. You may be amazed to learn that your new home might require seventy or eighty light bulbs. If so, is the seller going to leave them?

As you proceed with your investigation, look at every receptacle. Determine if they are the grounding type. Illustration #12 will help

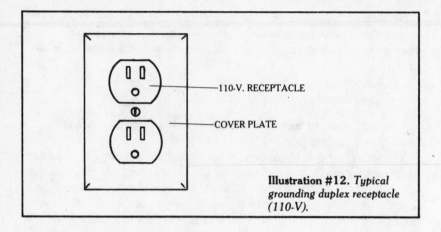

110-V. RECEPTACLE

COVER PLATE

Illustration #12. *Typical grounding duplex receptacle (110-V).*

you to identify them easily. If they are not, make a note to replace them. The owner is not required to do this, but you should upgrade this feature of the wiring.

You now need to inspect the main **electric service panel.** On the door of this panel is the identification plate. This plate will indicate total **amperage** available at the service panel. It should show a capacity of 60 amps, 100 amps, or more. This is one item where more is better.

Today's electric requirements demand a minimum 100-amp service. It is a good idea (now, and later when you move upstairs) to count all of the major appliances being used by the seller. Compare them with what you may be adding to the load. If you have more appliances or plan on increasing the number of electric appliances currently in the house, it may be necessary to increase the amperage of the existing panel. Upgrading the service panel (increasing the amperage input) is not the responsibility of the seller.

If you are thinking of increasing the panel from 60 amps to 100 amps, it may be well to raise it to 150 amps. The increased amperage of 50 amps is well worth the added cost while the work is being done. The cost to increase amperage of the service panel to 100 amps is in excess of $500. This should only be accomplished by a licensed electrician. Otherwise you may be in violation of the **building code.** For the additional 50 amps, the increase might only raise the total cost another $100. Although the fuse-type panel is less expensive, a circuit breaker service is preferable. It is easier to flip a switch than change a **fuse,** particularly in the dark.

In addition to determining amperage at the service panel, you will want to see if there are sub-panels. These are other electric-fused or circuit breaker-type boxes adjacent to the main service panel that are used to enlarge its capacity. It is not uncommon to see one or more sub-panels if the house has any age on it — even in houses less than ten years old. If the house is older than twenty years, you may see three, four, five, or more sub-panels. This is not necessarily bad as long as the size of the lead wire coming into the house is large enough to carry the additional requirements demanded by the sub-panels. Ideally, "the simpler the better" is a good criterion for electricity service. The cost of adding several sub-panels may not be much less than changing the main service panel in order to upgrade to the desired amperage.

You should be wary of electric lines that appear to have been run in disorderly fashion. It indicates that it was a do-it-yourself job and may not be as solidly grounded as it should be.

Wires that have been cut from a circuit and are hanging loose should not have bare ends. The ends of these wires should be wrapped with electrician's tape or be securely covered with **Romex wire nuts.**

It is a good idea to have more electric service available than you need at the beginning. It would be advisable to consider the cost of upgrading the electric service panel if in your analysis you've determined such upgrading is necessary. Do this before you make your offer of a purchase price. There are books available to you in most public libraries that will help you determine the necessity for increasing the amperage. Generally a 200-amp service will easily handle the requirements of a large family and a large house.

Insect Infestation

Before you finish the basement, ask about termite and bug protection. You may have already been advised by the real estate agent that an inspection has been made by a reliable firm. The firm should attest, after its inspection, that the house is free from bug-damaging infestation. Be certain that an inspection has been made and request a written copy of it. In some areas of the country a termite inspection is required by the lending institution before it approves the mortgage. Even today, many insurance companies are now insisting on a termite inspection before they underwrite the home owner's policy.

Many basement homes are partial, not full basements. The balance of the area underneath the house is crawl space or even slab construction. Crawl-space areas (their floors can be dirt, sand or concrete) are likely to breed vermin unless properly treated to prevent their infestation and growth.

You can make this inspection for bug-damaging infestation yourself. Illustration #13 will show you what you will be looking for. If the house is crawl-space construction, take your flashlight and screwdriver with you when you crawl through the access door. Move around the perimeter walls of the crawl space. Look for signs of "paths" traveling from the ground up these walls (and any pillars) to the wood **sill plate** located on the top of these walls. This illustration shows what you may be looking for.

The floor joists are attached to these plates. The "paths" will resemble a dry muddy-looking crust no larger in diameter than a wood #2 lead pencil. You also should use a screwdriver as a probe into the sill plate. If the screwdriver penetrates the wood easily, it is a danger signal. You may also see small penetration holes where wood beetles have entered. There may be some white splotches that indicate the presence of mold and mildew.

Even though the above may be present, these wood parts and the ground inside and out could have been treated for termites and no longer have any live infestation.

A word about "dry rot," which is a misnomer. Wood does not rot from being dry. This term is commonly used but what has happened is

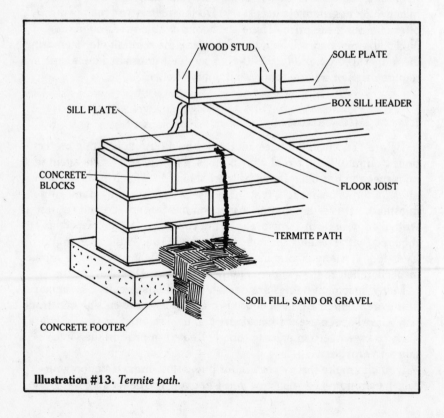

Illustration #13. *Termite path.*

that fungi and mildew have infected the wood and literally eaten away the lignum (the natural glue that holds the wood fibers together).

♠ ♠ ♠

Now that you've inspected the basement, it is time to go upstairs and inspect the rest of the house. How do you feel about what you found in your inspection? You may have discovered that you can easily live with some or most of what your investigation has revealed so far.

Utility Room:

The utility room may be inspected first if the house is the crawl-space, slab, or combination type.

The utility room, literally the location of the utilities — source of heat, electricity, and water in the house — can be as small as a closet or can be included in an area of the garage. Some houses have a narrow, deep room for utilities that is open at both ends with the placement of the water heater, furnace, and electric service panel in a row, one behind or beside the other. There is very little room for service work. A washer and dryer are frequently located in this same small area. The configuration of the room is not important as long as major repairs can be performed.

Occasionally you can find the main water shut-off valve in the utility room. It can usually be located at the floor level. Sometimes it will be in an obscure location, such as behind the water heater.

It is essential that an enclosed utility room have a **louvered door** on the opening to it. This louvered door allows the passage of free air exchange and eliminates the danger of combustion due to confining gas fumes.

Kitchen:

The kitchen is another critically important area that could be inspected next. Why don't you suggest that you would like to move to the kitchen? After all, there is more active time spent in the kitchen than in any other room in the house.

Begin by using your tape measure to determine the length of the usable cabinet space. Also measure the countertop to determine the amount of square feet of work space there is. Compare these dimensions to what you have in your present kitchen to see if you can get along with it. Don't count the sink. While it's true you use it, you don't set food or dishes on it or on the cooking top of the stove. These are to be left free for their intended use. In these calculations you are determining how much space you will have — for opening cans, mixing cakes, rolling out dough, buttering rolls, sifting flour, stirring vegetables, setting out finished cooked dishes, and generally doing the myriad tasks associated with preparing a meal. Many times, of course, these tasks are proceeding concurrently.

There are those in the family who may want to make a sandwich while you are spread out preparing a meal and your activities may require all of the space that is available. Ponder this point in your comparison. The size of your family now or in the future is important in determining the size of the cabinet and counter space you need. If you are coming from an apartment or a very small house, you may be overwhelmed to find six or seven feet of usable counter space.

What might be overlooked is the refrigerator you are bringing with you. Does the door of yours swing in the same direction as the owner's? Many late model single-door refrigerators can be adapted from right swing to left swing and vice versa. Check yours to see if that is possible. If it is, there will be screwholes on the top of the door and the box (they probably will be covered with plastic grommets) for re-mounting the door. If not, perhaps the one the owner has can be negotiated. Does the color of yours go well or clash with these new surroundings?

While you are looking at the cabinets, really examine them. Make a note about the age of the cabinets, the type, and brand. By opening and closing all of the doors and drawers of the cabinets, you will find the kind of use they have been subjected to. The doors and drawers may no longer fit well. Are there many grease stains in the cooking area? If so, start thinking again about bug infestation. Don't fail to ask about the kind of bug treatment the seller uses.

If the corner base and wall cabinets are situated at right angles, are they equipped with **lazy Susans?** If not, they contain much wasted space. Wasted space in kitchen cabinets is space where there is not easy access to what is stored. Without easy access to this space you will store many things in them and, if you're like most people, you will forget what you stored. Therefore, you should consider lazy Susans in the cabinets a plus for the house.

Storage space in the kitchen is very necessary and should be carefully considered in the light of your lifestyle. You may be a person who keeps more than a three or four day supply of canned goods. This requires a minimum of 64 cubic feet of storage space for a family of four. You may do a great deal of baking and cooking that demands a wide variety of devices. You may entertain extensively (or plan to do so) and have storage needs for additional crystal, china, linen, and silverware.

The age of the appliances in the kitchen is an important consideration. Manufacturers have two categories for appliances: minor and major. Toasters, irons, coffee makers, etc., are included in the minor category. Stoves, refrigerators, dishwashers, etc., are major appliances. It is difficult, if not impossible, to find repair parts for minor appliances. In defense of the manufacturers, they realize that the cost of labor to repair them, in most instances, is greater than that of purchasing new ones. Replacement parts for many major electric appliances are manufactured up to ten years after the last date of manufacture for a given model.

Major electric appliances have a normal operating dependability of six to seven years for the top-of-the-line models. Contractor-builder models have only five years or less. For example, the dishwasher in a particular house is seven years old. The seller tells you he has never had to repair it. Look out! The formula explained above shows that the dishwasher may need repair soon after you move in. When the seal and motor fail (this is likely at the age of this dishwasher), you're in for a major repair bill. At that point it would even be wise to consider replacing the dishwasher.

How does one determine the true age of an electric appliance? Every electric appliance has a metal identification plate permanently attached to it. This plate is easily located for quick reference so that an identifying model number can be established for the ordering of repair parts. You have only to call your local supplier of appliance parts and identify the brand name and model number for him to give you the year of manufacture. Gas appliances will not have this identification plate because gas cooking appliances rarely require service.

Is there a garbage disposal? Continuous-feed is preferable to batch-feed, which takes longer to dispose of large quantities of food. Inquire about its age. Start it up with the cold water turned on and listen to the disposal run. It should operate quietly unless there are some food particles left from its last operation.

Turn on the cooking exhaust vent at the stove. Listen to it run. It should be relatively quiet, i.e., no knocking of the motor while it is running. Incidentally, cooking exhaust vent hoods, although not major appliances, have replacement parts for them available for ten years or so.

You will want to make a list of all of the gas and electric appliances that remain with the real estate as part of the asking price. These should be enumerated in the real estate agent's listing. An authorized appraisal made of the real estate will list these appliances also. If an appraisal has not been made, you should insist that this be done prior to your offer to purchase. Unless you are going to pay for the real estate without a mortgage, the lending institution will insist upon one being made and charge you for it. Either way you will pay for one!

Have you looked at and operated the kitchen faucet? You should, and as with all the faucets in the house be certain to operate both the cold and the hot. It has happened that inoperable hot water was not discovered until after the buyer had moved in. Look for telltale signs of corrosion around the base of the faucet where it sits on the sink. When you turn on the hot or cold water, is there leakage around either the base or the top of the spout or handles? If so, the **"O" rings** are defective and need to be replaced. Of course, the situation could be so bad that only a new faucet will correct it. The "O" ring repair will cost about $30 if you hire a plumber to do it. Should the faucet need replacing, it will cost much more. An "O" ring repair is a simple procedure for a plumber who probably will have the correct size in his truck as well as the expertise to do the job without damage to the faucet. If you do it, you will need to shut off the water, remove the defective "O" ring, take it to the hardware store, and *hope* that the store has its replacement.

While you are at the kitchen sink with your flashlight, stoop down and open the cabinet door. Be sure and explain before you do this that you are so interested in this house you want to make certain everything is in good working order before you commit yourself.

You want to look at the drainpipes. Are they pitted, corroded? Is tape wrapped around them? Since you just ran the water, there will be a visible sign of moisture on the floor in the back of the cabinet if the faucet leaks. If the drainpipes are bad, you may even detect moisture on them as well.

While you are viewing this area under the sink, if there is a garbage disposal and/or dishwasher, there should be a **fused electric switch box** mounted on the side or back of the cabinet. (See illustration #14.) It is important that this box be present. An overload on the circuit by either appliance will cause a **short circuit** (interruption in the flow of electricity). A fuse will blow, or it will trip a **circuit breaker.** Having this box at the kitchen sink area is a convenience as well as a necessity. If the electric supply to these appliances has been tapped in from another circuit without installing this fused box at the sink, damage to other appliances on that line could result. This is especially true if there is a microwave oven being used on the same line. Each of these appliances should be powered by their own circuit. Not to have this fused box is indicative that the appliance was installed by an unknowl-

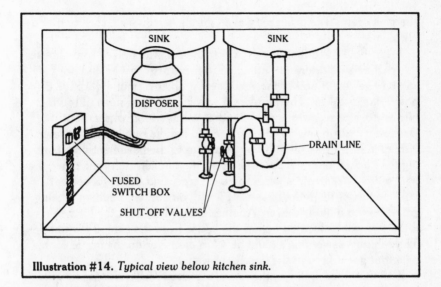

Illustration #14. *Typical view below kitchen sink.*

edgeable person. It would be another good place to make a note. To properly install what has been explained as a necessity would cost $75 or more.

One last thing to inspect while you're down looking under the sink are the water lines. Do they have **shut-off valves?** No? Then every time there are repairs made on the faucet or those water lines, the main water shut-off valve will need to be closed. This will shut off the entire water supply to the house. When a plumber services that faucet he will, in all probability, install shut-off valves. They should have been installed originally.

Now stand up and insert one of the **basket strainers** in the sink and lock it into position to close off the drain. Half fill the sink with cold water. Release the basket strainer to see how clear or clogged the drain is. If there is an automatic dishwasher, the water will probably drain quickly. The dishwasher forces out seven gallons of water when it drains. Because of pumping or forcing out of this water, the daily use of a dishwasher is a big help in maintaining an open drain.

Of course, if the drain line is broken underground and roots are growing in it, then the dishwasher can not be the primary mover of food particles, grease, and soap accumulation through the drain. Should this condition exist, calling a plumber to rout the line is only a temporary measure. A broken drain line underground must be repaired at some point in time. This is the reason you are checking the drain — to determine how well it reacts to the release of the water you ran in the sink. No dishwasher? Without one you may experience a sluggish drain. The drain may even gurgle at you — a sure sign of a problem.

Just a note of caution here. During the construction of some houses the kitchen sink drain was attached to the **storm sewer** and not the sanitary sewer. Many of these had few problems until a garbage disposal was installed. Then the drain was in continual need of routing because a storm sewer is not intended to have food wastes sent through it. Storm sewers are designed to handle non-bacterial water. You can detect this situation by returning to the basement and locating the kitchen drain. If the drain from the kitchen sink runs down the wall of the basement, is joined by a 2″ pipe, and then proceeds at right angles through the basement wall, you can lay odds on it being connected to a storm sewer. Another clue will be that the kitchen drain line will be located across the house from the sanitary sewer line. The sanitary sewer line should be 4″ in diameter on the inside of the pipe that goes through the basement wall.

If all the other drains in the house are emptying with ease, it will become obvious that the kitchen drain and the other drains are not connected. The exception could be if the kitchen drain is connected to the sanitary sewer and a break in the sanitary sewer line exists underground between where it leaves the house and where it connects the sanitary sewer line. At some point this situation will have to be corrected. If the problem is outside it will require digging to the break, repairing it, and refilling the hole. Should the kitchen drain be connected to a storm sewer, it will then require cutting the drain before it proceeds through the wall, plugging the cut, rerouting the drain, and connecting it to the sanitary sewer line. This type of job performed by a licensed plumber can cost from $150 to several hundreds more.

A proper-acting drain will react positively when you release the basket strainer. The water will immediately begin to show an eddy in the center of the drain while it is emptying and, nearing its completion, will give off a sucking sound. That is a healthy action and one you should require. Don't do it now, just mark the appropriate place on the checklist.

🏠 🏠 🏠

You've given the kitchen a thorough inspection. What you have learned has either pleased or distressed you. The kitchen is generally the area of the house that receives most attention, simply because there is more active time spent in the kitchen than in any other room in the house. People are realizing this more and more, which may account for enormous growth of the kitchen remodeling business since the late 70s. If you are beginning to lean favorably toward the purchase of the house you are previewing, you may already be considering updating the kitchen.

Bathroom:

It is now time to take a very hard look at the bathroom. If there is more than one, use the same criteria established here for all. Do not (I repeat do not) hurry through the inspection of the bathroom, especially since there are things that can be overlooked. Even buyers who are purchasing their second or third house may overlook them.

Where is the **plumbing access door?** Many people do not know what the term means. It is a small opening in the wall at the drain end of the bathtub that provides an opening to facilitate service on the tub drain and faucet. It usually is 14″ wide by 24″ high with a molding surrounding it for the sake of appearance as well as stability. Many houses do not have an access door. When (not if) it becomes necessary to repair the bathtub drain this door may need to be built.

In many split-level homes, as well as in other styles, bathtubs are situated so that it is an added cost to get to the drain when repair is needed. In others the access door will need to be cut into the wall, which may be in the foyer, hall, or dining area, or occasionally in a stairwell. If the tub faces a closet there is no problem in making an access door. The same is true of a bedroom where a piece of furniture can be set in front of it. Those tubs that face a shower or another tub on the other side of the wall can become a costly repair bill.

Be certain that you establish whether there is a plumbing access door. It will not be offensive to ask the seller where it is. However, he may not be aware of its presence or know what you are talking about.

Is the bathroom equipped with an electric exhaust vent? It is very important for every bathroom to have one of these vents. Unfortunately, this is often not the case. Removing offensive odors from the bathroom is only a secondary function of the bath vent. Its primary function is to remove moisture. There is a huge amount of moisture in the air during bathing. Mildew is caused by the penetration of abnormal amounts of moisture into the various types of existing materials in the bathroom.

If mildew exists and there is an exhaust fan in the bathroom, it indicates that the fan was either not used or occasionally used and even then not long enough. It also could have so much lint in it that it will not run or is broken. The success of moisture removal in the bathroom depends on the exhaust fan being used every time bathing occurs. And the fan should be operated long enough. Long enough means operating the exhaust fan during and for ten to fifteen minutes following a bath or shower. This is most successfully accomplished by wiring the fan to a timer switch.

While you are considering the tub/shower area, look at the walls inside the tub area. What do you see — ceramic tile, plastic tile, **fiberglass tub surround,** a painted wall, a window — or is it a one-piece unit of tub and wall?

Take one thing at a time. First of all, if there is a window in the tub area, it's a big mistake. Even if there isn't a shower in the tub, there still is a large amount of hot steam rising from the tub during bathing.

Moisture constantly attacking **wood miter joints** and other loose-fitting joints will take its toll. Deterioration of a window in the tub area can be slight to very severe. You are making the inspection, so make the determination yourself. Be certain to look very closely at this window.

If the walls are covered with ceramic tile, you should lean over and firmly tap your finger on the center of the tiles around the faucet, tub filler (see illustration #15), and the lower part of the long wall that the

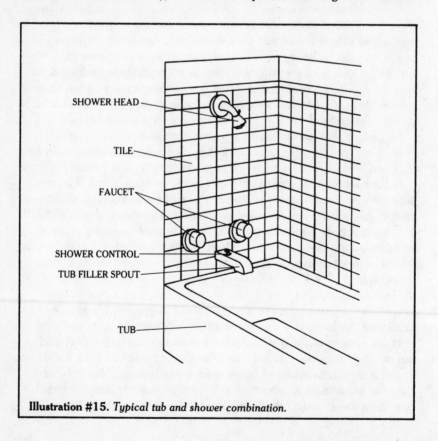

SHOWER HEAD

TILE

FAUCET

SHOWER CONTROL

TUB FILLER SPOUT

TUB

Illustration #15. *Typical tub and shower combination.*

tub rests against near the front corner. Should a tile be loose, you will hear a little vibration, a "clicking" sound. When you hear this sound, not only are the tiles loose but it could also mean wall damage behind them. This can be a more serious problem than meets the eye. If the pattern or color of tile is no longer manufactured, repair and replacement can be more than a simple repair job.

Now you may reconsider the leak referred to earlier on page 17. Many bathroom shower areas leak for one or more of these reasons: 1) The faucet and tub filler spout may need caulking; 2) the tile on the walls may be loose, allowing water to get in behind; and 3) water may be leaking from under the track of the tub or shower enclosure, be it a door or a curtain. All of these are caused by water splashing during showering and by the great pressure created by hot moisture, which causes great expansion. At first there is very minute penetration by this moisture. Little by little it gets worse, expanding to the point that it lets in large amounts of moisture. Subsequently a leak becomes apparent one day on the ceiling of the room below the shower. You can see why it would be nearly impossible to detect this leak without duplicating the showering activity of a bather.

Now back to the problems of tile and, also problematic, the brand of tile. While you may find a close enough color or contrast that would suit you, new tiles may not fit unless they are the same brand. Minor differences of size, thickness, and color exist among manufacturers. Consider making a note at this point that you may be in for a tub-area remodeling job. Unless the tub faucet is very new, you should replace it while this area is being remodeled. With a fiberglass tub surround, a new faucet, and the labor, you are looking at a cost of $650 and up.

Walls covered with plastic tile should *not* be tapped on. They will pop off if they are loose, and you will be liable. However, with a close visual inspection you can determine their worth. Plastic wall tile has not been manufactured since 1970, so don't even consider repairing or replacing it. Choose the fiberglass tub surround as explained above. It makes good economic sense and reduces your maintenance costs to a minimum.

If the walls outside the tub area are papered, look for loose edges and seams. Moisture attacks even the best wallpaper. It's another good reason to have an exhaust and use it.

Look around the room carefully for broken tiles, bubbled and blistered paint, broken or cracked walls or ceiling, cracked mirror or glass, sufficient towel bars, etc. Be alert to all the little things. Even the aesthetics of the room may "cry" for a change. They represent dollars that can add up very quickly to a large amount.

Should the bathroom floor be covered with ceramic tile, in all likelihood it too is coming loose. Check it out and make a note. This is no small repair bill. Sometimes there will be carpeting installed over ceramic tile, linoleum, or vinyl tile. This carpeting can become moisture laden, thereby creating a mildew odor and discoloration in specific areas. Put your hand on the carpeting and feel for moisture.

There shouldn't be much to checking out a toilet, right? Wrong. You will want to do more than flush it to see if it takes the water away with authority. Remove the tank lid and gently set it aside. Flush the toilet. You may be surprised to find a worn-out **ball cock** and flush handle. See how quickly it refills and time it to see if it takes longer than two minutes. If it does, the ball cock needs to be at least cleaned out if not replaced. And yet it could be caused by mineral build-up in the water supply line.

After the toilet has refilled, replace the lid and raise the seat to see that the water shuts off completely. With your flashlight held at an angle against the side of the bowl at the water level, you can see if water is leaking. If it is, you will notice a very slight disturbance of water in the bowl. You may also hear a "hissing" sound like a small amount of air escaping. This indicates water is passing through ever so slightly. Repairing this could easily run $50 or more.

Lean over to see if there is a shut-off valve for the toilet. It wouldn't hurt to check the china for any cracks. Now with your hands grab each side of the toilet bowl, and attempt to rock it sideways but not too strongly. If it is loose from the closet collar, you're in for an additional repair bill in excess of $50. Should the **closet collar,** or floor flange, be the reason for the toilet's being loose, that $50 repair bill could quickly jump to over a hundred dollars. And if the floor is soft or spongy around the toilet, it is important to replace that while the job is being done. Again this will increase the repair bill.

You haven't looked at the lavatory. Do so now with the same "eye" you used to inspect the kitchen plumbing at the sink. Look at the faucet. Run both hot and cold water. Close off the drain, partially fill the sink with water, release the water, and check the drain for sluggishness. Then look below to see what running the water caused. Remember you're looking for faucet leaks and deterioration, drain leaks, and the presence of shut-off valves.

When you've finished the lavatory, just turn around and check the drain in the tub for sluggishness. You may learn that the trip lever that operates the drain in an open or closed position is broken. Replacing that lever assembly is around a $50 job plus cleaning the drain if it is sluggish. Be sure to activate the shower control. If there is one it will be located on the **tub filler spout** (refer to illustration #15) or in the faucet above. It may or may not work properly. When the control is activated water should not come from the tub filler spout at all while the water is running, but should come instead from the shower head. Check it out to make certain that it works properly.

Wow, what a journey this has been so far! It's a good bet that the seller or the real estate agent never expected to have someone as knowledgeable as you inspect the premises. And you're not through yet, not by a long way.

Bedroom:

It is now time to move to each bedroom. Use the criteria established here in one for all of them. Just before you enter the room, look at the casing. That's the wood trim around the door frame (what many people still refer to as "facing"). A common problem in many homes is the separation of the miter joints at the top. Be sure and check this. If there is a separation, there may also be a crack of varying widths on the wall (see illustration #16), running at an angle toward the ceiling. This indicates an abnormal movement in the wall. It could be that it was improperly framed around the door.

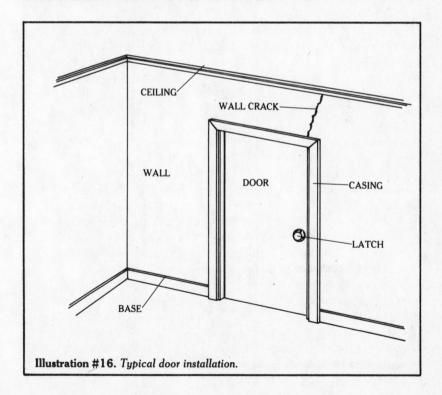

Illustration #16. *Typical door installation.*

This could also be a moisture problem. If it is, it will be noticeable especially at each bathroom door on one or both sides. The house isn't falling apart, but it will be a recurring defect until the cause is corrected. Be certain to check all casing mitered joints and the walls above each door throughout the house on both sides.

While you are checking swinging hinged doors, make certain they close securely. Often a door won't close securely because of the defect described above. Another clue to this is that the door binds somewhere around the frame when it is closed and opened. Notice whether the paint or stain on the door frame appears to have been rubbed off at a spot or two. You will know this condition exists without having to open or close the doors. Sometimes this bind is caused by nothing more than loose hinges. You should determine if this is the cause of the door rubbing the frame as it closes. It may be just that simple.

You may find, especially where children have been roughhousing, that the door frame is split above and below the door **strike plate**. (See illustration #17.) The door strike plate is the metal piece that is screwed to the frame after the frame has been chiseled out to accept

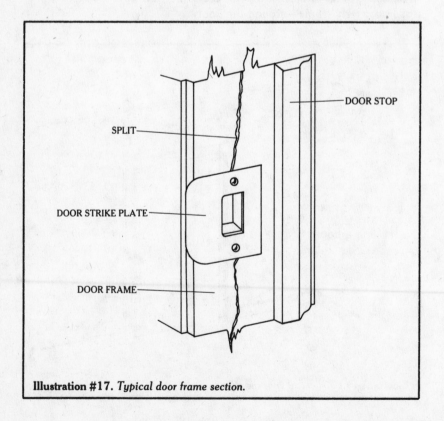

Illustration #17. *Typical door frame section.*

it. It allows the strike of the latch to secure the door. To repair or re-place this is a $100+ job. That will not include the repainting needed.

Remember to check the light switch. Some bedrooms do not have ceiling lights. Instead, the switch operates one wall receptacle. If your furniture will fit the room the same way as this occupant has it arranged, fine. What happens is that the switch operating a wall receptacle is meant to be used for a bedside lamp, so that it can be switched off at the lamp while in bed rather than getting up to turn off the ceiling fixture.

Windows:

Do the windows operate easily? What is the material used in their construction? Is it wood, aluminum, steel, or vinyl? Do they have to be painted and do they need paint now? Do they show many coats of paint? Do they lock securely? Open the windows unless it's too much of a hassle, and tap on the center of each sill. Do they sound hollow? Any broken or cracked glass? Whatever you find, be certain to check out the window casing the same as you did the doors.

If the windows are old enough to be the type operated with **weights and cords,** you must consider these as your biggest contributor to heat loss. Even the lack of insulation in the ceiling and sidewalls does not rank as high in energy loss as poor windows. A major manufac-turer of quality wood windows uses this poignant phrase in its advertis-ing: "Only the rich can afford cheap windows." That is true and only increases in soundness with the ever growing energy costs. You should consider as a liability each wood window with weights and cords used as **sash balances** and deduct at least $50 per window.

It may be advisable for you to consider **replacement windows** to upgrade the house. Certainly it is not the obligation of the seller to replace the windows he might have been living with for many years. But buying a house with loose-fitting windows might be compared with purchasing an automobile that gets only four miles to the gallon. You certainly wouldn't consider doing that anymore.

Another real thief of heat is either the steel or the aluminum win-dow. Unless the aluminum window has a **thermal barrier** between the inside and outside part of the frame and a thermal barrier between each sash, it will transmit an enormous amount of cold air in the win-ter. In severe cold weather, frost will appear on it on the inside of the house. The sash and frame will frost on the inside of the house too. As the frost thaws, water will collect on the **window stool** and run down the wall. Make another deduction of $50 per window for this type. In the hot months, aluminum windows (what is being referred to here are the **prime windows,** not storm windows) will be one cause for additional work load on the air-conditioning system. The explanation for this phenomenon is that heat seeks cold.

If the windows are steel, the situation is more critical than with aluminum windows. Steel windows have outlived their time. Not only does the metal transmit the cold, but this type of window needs continual reputtying and painting. In addition, they never close tightly enough. Definitely consider replacing them, although it is a large job. Depending on their size, it would be conservative to estimate the replacement cost to average $400 per window including materials and labor.

There is one wood window that you may happen upon that was a superior type with its own block-and-tackle-type balance — the Curtis window. Except for the balance it looks no different from other wood windows. These windows still exist in homes today and when you find them you will probably see that they are in excellent condition.

In some areas of the country, cold weather is not a factor to be reckoned with. Replacing the steel or aluminum window there would be unnecessary. In these same geographic areas the jalousie window may be found. These windows have aluminum frames and are filled with many narrow, single slats of glass operated by a crank similar to an awning-type window. These windows are popular throughout the **Sunbelt.**

While windows and their energy efficiency are the subject of discussion here, it is necessary to explain the various types of sash balances used in wood windows. Not all wood windows are operated by weights and cords.

There are three basic styles of sash balances: 1) spring-loaded; 2) block and tackle; and 3) side mount tension. The spring-loaded style has variations of spiral, coated springs, and nylon twine. Block and tackle style is simply a stainless steel band that coils one way and then the other through a pulley as the window is lowered or raised. The side mount tension is an aluminum or stainless steel track on which the sash operates. Only one of the side tracks has the tension, which is adjustable. It is necessary for it to be adjustable so that the tension can be changed as the atmospheric pressure and temperature changes.

Do the window treatments (drapes, blinds, venetians, shutters, sheers, valances, etc.) remain with the house? How many holes are visible, from where you stand, in the wall or casing that held other hardware at different times and heights? If there are many holes it's a telltale sign that the existing hardware is probably loose. You'll have puttying and painting to do when you move in — or before. If there are shutters hung at the windows, make certain they are securely hung and close properly. Also make certain there are no broken slats.

Closets:

The closet is next. How wide and deep (front-to-back) is it? Closet doors fall into one of three categories: swinging hinged, **by-passing** (referred to by some as sliding), and **bi-folding.** The latter can be either wood or steel. Boisterous play in a bedroom can be the cause for damage to the hardware of either by-pass or bi-fold. You should open and close each of these doors to determine their smooth operation.

In all probability you are being escorted through the house by the seller or a real estate agent. Presumably that real estate agent has already determined how well or how poorly these closet doors operate, but do not take it for granted. Assure yourself — it's really your only protection.

Is there a storage shelf above the hanging rod in the closet? Is this shelf bowed or damaged so that it will require replacement by you? Is the hanging rod bent so far out of shape that it too will need to be replaced?

In many bedrooms you cannot tell much about the carpet, because the room is too full of furniture and decorations to determine much. In fact, it is unlikely that you will be able to see very much of it. Should the carpet be older than ten years it may be advisable to consider recarpeting. An adequate carpeting job in a bedroom will cost several hundred dollars or more depending upon the quality of carpeting you select. The price should include removal, clean-up, pad, carpeting, and labor.

Before you leave the room, look at the paint on the woodwork, ceiling, and walls. This is one of the reasons to inspect in the daytime when more defects are exposed than you'll ever see in the evening. Check out the seams of the wallpaper, for they may be coming loose. If the walls are paneled you may not be able to tell much because of furniture and decorations.

Every house has defects, whether it has been lived in or not. In your inspection you are trying to find all of them so that you can make a dollar evaluation of the cost to you of repairing or replacing them. Also many homes have been tastefully touched up to make them appealing. It is advantageous to the seller to have the house looking its best when it is presented on the market for sale. You simply must not be overwhelmed and swayed by these aesthetics.

Floors:

Did you notice the floors squeaking as you walked on them? Whether they are carpeted or not, this can be a constant source of irritation to you once you have moved in. Loose flooring can be attributed to the absence of **sub-flooring** under the finished floor, or **bridging.** (This is either wood or steel braces that have been anchored between floor joists and installed on the diagonal, appearing as an "X".) Illustration #18 best shows this. You probably noticed the joists while you were in the basement or the crawl space. It is rare, but it has been noticed on some inspections that the bridging was never nailed to the floor joists. Sometimes the bridging has come loose due to severe damage from floods or earthquakes.

Whatever books and "old-timers" say, a squeaky floor cannot be cured without removing the old and doing what should have been done originally.

In the case of some older and larger Victorian homes, however, a tongue-and-groove **poplar** sub-floor was laid and nailed diagonally to the floor joists. Deadening felt paper was placed on top of it, and the hardwood floor nailed at right angles to the floor joists on top of this felt paper.

This type of construction has held its stability even to this day. As you tread this type of floor construction, you'll get a really warm feeling of stability. Rarely is this feeling of stability found in today's construction, even in the finer homes.

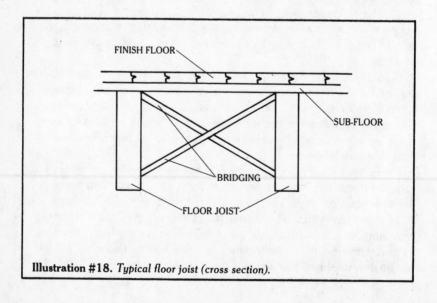

Illustration #18. *Typical floor joist (cross section).*

Another cause for squeaking is the use of ⅜″ hardwood flooring as a finish floor. Even though sub-flooring and bridging is properly used, the finish flooring is too thin to withstand the test of the time, temperature, and humidity changes that occur in all houses.

Concerning temperature and humidity, it is important to maintain stability in both of these throughout the house. Maintaining a humidity level between 40% and 50% and a temperature of 68 to 70 degrees will ensure the stability of the building materials and wood furniture present in the house. It will also greatly reduce the static electricity so prevalent in today's homes because of the increasing use of plastic in nearly everything that is manufactured. Large temperature and humidity changes greatly affect the expansion and contraction of all materials.

Floor Covering:

Kitchens and bath floors are frequently covered with linoleum or plastic composition tile. What you will be looking for are seam edges that have come loose and are beginning to curl. When these seams are in the traffic pattern, people trip over them and make the damage more severe. Repair costs can run from a simple cleaning of the area below the curl and re-cementing with a good contact cement, to the replacement of the entire floor covering. The reason for replacement rather than repair is that the curl loses some of its elasticity and becomes brittle. It may already show signs of cracking or crazing.

Pure vinyl, asbestos, rubber, and vinyl-asbestos floor tiles have been successfully used over the years. A great many homes where these types of tile are found will be in good shape. The inherent need for wax on these floor coverings is a never-ending job and expense. More recently manufactured linoleum yard goods (since 1980) requires no waxing. Inspect this and note it on your checklist.

Stairways:

You may have had an occasion by this time to use other stairs besides the basement stairs in the house. Give them the same critical tests you gave the stairs to the basement. Are they stable? Is there a well-secured handrail? Carpet on the stairs receives heavy traffic, which results in fraying of the landing edges of the treads. Check for this!

If the lower third of a stairwell is open, it should have a **balustrade** for protection. Without one it is an invitation to serious injury for young and old alike. (See illustration #19)

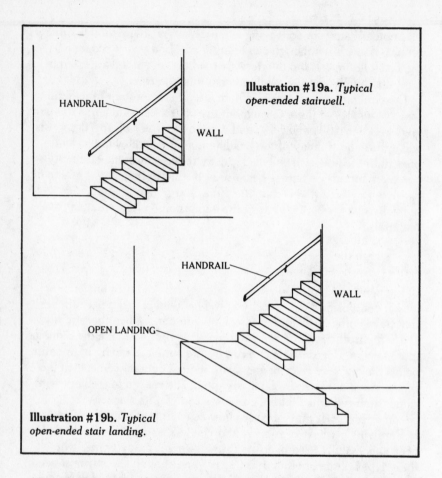

Illustration #19a. *Typical open-ended stairwell.*

HANDRAIL

WALL

HANDRAIL

WALL

OPEN LANDING

Illustration #19b. *Typical open-ended stair landing.*

Stairs without carpeting tend to be slippery. This is a danger not only to children but to adults as well. If this situation exists in the house you are inspecting, be sure to make a note of it. It may be something you will want to correct before you move in.

Attic:

If you are on the second floor or in a single level house with a crawl-through door, **scuttle hole** or **disappearing stairs,** do your best to get a peek into the attic. It's simply amazing what you may uncover unless, of course, the attic is filled with memorabilia, suit-cases, boxes, Christmas decorations, etc.

Many times getting into the attic is not easy. Sometimes it requires standing on the top rung of a ladder and physically lifting yourself with your hands and arms through the scuttle hole. The scuttle hole is frequently located in a closet. Usually in an attached garage the scuttle hole or disappearing stairs will be in its ceiling. The attic is always dusty and if it is an older house (older here refers to pre-World War II), there may be an accumulation of soot caused by coal-burning furnaces.

Loose insulation that was poured or blown into the attic may cause you to cough a little because the fibers when disturbed are very easily inhaled. To avoid breathing these irritating fibers you can include, among your "tools" for making an inspection, an inexpensive **respirator.** You can pick up a respirator in most hardware stores in the paint department for a couple of dollars.

You may also have difficulty getting around in an attic that is not floored. It is important to be very careful where you step in an unfloored attic. You certainly do not want to accidentally run your foot through the ceiling. Nevertheless, the trip into the attic is worth your inconvenience. If you do not wish to make that inspection, hire someone to do it for you.

You may discover in a house with gables that the vents are not protected from an invasion by birds. In the winter, birds roost in these openings. In the spring they make excellent places to build their nests. Some vents have a large enough opening (2"–3") that even squirrels will use. Covering the opening on the inside with ¼" galvanized mesh wire eliminates this problem. This is a job you can do yourself. To have it done can cost in excess of $100.

With your trusty flashlight you may view a "sea" of insulation in the ceiling of the house, or you may not. There will be wiring exposed in the attic — that's okay. The **transformer** that operates the doorbell may also be installed up there. What you really want to see (it's the only way to find out) is whether there are water stains running down the **rafters,** around the plumbing and attic vents, or around the chimney. If you find this situation, simply ask the seller, "Have you corrected your roof leaks yet?" He may answer that he was unaware of any, which may be the truth. This situation may have occurred sometime in the past, was corrected, and has not happened since.

You will find that some roof leaks occur only when a severe rainstorm blows from one certain direction. They may occur only during a "southwesterly" occurring in late spring or summer. Or it may be just the opposite — leaks appear during a storm driven from the northwest and occurring in the late fall and winter.

If you don't view a "sea" of insulation in the attic, it means that heat passes through the ceiling and subsequently through the roof. The insulation needn't be the blown-in or loose type; it could be batt or roll type instead. In areas of the country where there is a snow accumulation it is easy to detect houses that have too little or no insulation in the attics. You have only to drive around your own neighborhood to see this. Snow does not accumulate on roofs where there is sufficient heat penetration from the ceiling of the house.

Who can afford to heat the outside of the house as well as the inside? To have the attic insulated with loose blown-in insulation varies in cost according to the size of the attic and the thickness of the insulation. A safe figure to start with is $300. If you prefer to have batt or roll insulation installed, the cost will increase.

You've inspected the basement, kitchen, bath, bedrooms, windows, doors, floors, ceilings, walls, stairs, paint, wallpaper, ceramic tile, water lines, drain lines, water heater, floor drain, furnace, casing, carpeting, switches, receptacles, light fixtures, appliances, wiring, attic, insulation, and checked for roof leaks. Are you ready to go outside? *Not so fast!* There are a few other things you need to check out inside the house before you can move outside.

Fireplace:

Is there a fireplace in the house? Is it original or was it installed later during the fireplace "mania"? Does the fireplace have a **steel insert** burner? These inserts come in a variety of face fronts. If there isn't an insert of this kind or a good set of glass doors to seal off the mouth of the fireplace, the fireplace is another big heat spender.

The **damper** in the fireplace allows fumes, sparks, and smoke to escape. From an energy conservation standpoint, fireplaces without some sort of sealed front are undesirable. They are silent fuel thieves. When the damper is open, which of course it must be when a fire is going, the heat is being removed from the room. It literally sucks the air, cold as well as warm, from the room.

Without a steel fireplace insert, it is important to check the mortar around the inside of the fireplace with your bright flashlight. Look for crumbling and softness of the mortar by probing with your screwdriver. Loose mortar in the firebox can be dangerous. If this is the situation, you should not burn anything in the fireplace. Plan on installing a steel fireplace insert.

You may also notice a blackening around the top of the facing of the brick or stone lintel. This is an indication that the flue may not draw strongly enough to remove all of the smoke. Or it could be that a fire was started in the fireplace without first opening the damper. However, this should generally have occurred only once, and the blackening would not be severe.

For energy cost effectiveness a fireplace needs an insert. A steel insert, depending on design, will cost from $400 to $700. Because the damper must be left open permanently when there is an insert, there will be the additional cost of filling in around it to seal off the small cracks surrounding the opening. These are a result of the insert not being the exact size of the fireplace opening. Just make a note and decide on it later.

In its defense, the fireplace is very comforting and creates a nostalgic feeling. Some fireplaces were originally built with tempered glass doors installed tightly on the front with the damper control arm placed through the front of the fireplace for convenience of operation. When you find one of these it is a big plus for the house and eliminates the need to reach up in the blackened fireplace and operate a soot-covered damper control.

For some people a fireplace is a luxury that outweighs many of its disadvantages. Simple safety precautions should be observed in the use of a fireplace. Sparks from a burning log can cause a disastrous fire, hence the need for a spark screen.

If you don't inspect the **flue** or if it appears questionable, hire someone to do this for you or make it one more entry on your checklist.

Safety:

At this point it is time to touch on smoke and heat detectors and locks. Until as recently as 1978, smoke and heat detectors were not given much consideration. The surge for their installation is largely attributable to devastating fires occurring in mobile homes and trailers. Since that time a lot of money has been spent nationally to alert people to the advantages of installing them in strategic areas of the home.

There is no doubt that if one of these alarms is activated in an emergency it can help save your life and perhaps those of your loved ones. It can, that is, if it actually works. Most alarm systems you find of this type are battery operated. The alarm is only as good as the battery. Periodically, it should be test-activated to determine its ability to function. Try to activate any that you see in your inspection. The fact that these may or may not operate should not be viewed as a drawback.

Today everyone should know the importance of door locks. You'd be surprised to learn about the number of entrance door locks that are not secure when the door is shut. It is very important to assure yourself that all door locks operate properly.

A plus in this respect is the entrance that has a **deadbolt lock** installed. Illustration #20 shows both types of deadbolt locks, single and double. A double-locking deadbolt lock requires the use of a key on either side of the door to unlock it. This means that a burglar cannot break the glass in the door and then reach in and manipulate the turn button on the other side to unlock the door. The single-locking deadbolt lock gives the burglar the chance to manipulate the turn button.

While a double-locking deadbolt lock is a plus for security, it also poses a problem. The person inside does not have quick egress from the house because the lock must be opened from the inside with the key. If there is a fire, this can be a point for panic, especially if the key is not handy at the door or if it is dark inside when the emergency arises. Remember always to keep a key handy inside near any door with a double-locking dead bolt installed on it.

If, on the other hand, a single-locking deadbolt lock is operated with a key on the outside and a turn button on the inside, it loses part of its purpose for security. It is recommended that a single-locking deadbolt lock be installed on entrance doors that are solid without glass. For those entrances that do have glass it is recommended that a double-locking deadbolt lock be installed.

Note: If you have one or more electric smoke detectors in your home, you may qualify for a lower classification on your homeowner's insurance policy. Check with your insurance agent. This also applies to dead-bolt locks and burglar alarms.

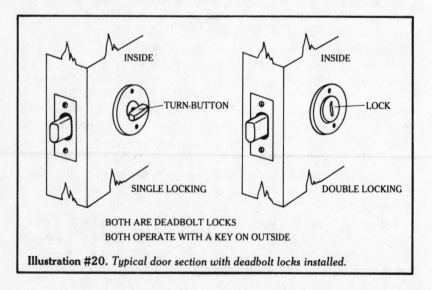

Illustration #20. *Typical door section with deadbolt locks installed.*

PART TWO
OUTSIDE

2 · OUTSIDE

Hopefully, you have chosen a dry day to make this inspection. A rainy day, however, would give you the chance to inspect the attic for roof leaks and the gutters for proper drainage.

You will now want to start a systematic inspection of siding, windows, guttering, downspouts, roofing, vents, roof edge, gable ends, porches, railings, walks, driveways, **caulking**, weatherstripping, **sill cocks, soffit,** paint, outdoor lighting, outbuildings and their components, and landscaping.

Roof:

You *can* start at the top and work your way down. To get the ideal view of the roof, get a ladder and climb up on it. Looks can be very deceiving from the ground. Here you may use your binoculars. Find out how old the roofing is. The real estate agent should have this information in the listing of the house. Make certain that the agent's information is correct.

Is the roofing asphalt the composition roll type? Is it shingles of wood, slate, aluminum, or asphalt composition? Perhaps the roof is covered with a glazed or terra cotta tile. Let us assume that you are looking at an asphalt composite type of shingle covered with a **mica surface.** A standard type would be 235# shingles. This type of roofing has a life expectancy of twenty years. The so-called "architectural-type" shingles have a longer life expectancy because they are much thicker than the standard 235# shingles. You have only to subtract the age of the roofing to determine the balance of its life expectancy.

Presumably a twenty-year guaranteed roofing will last that long.
Depending on the geographic location of the house you are inspecting,
this may or may not be true. Subjection to extreme temperatures, heat
and cold, pelting rainstorms, hail, sleet, and ice can be cause for a
reduction in the life expectancy of asphalt composition roofing.

You will want to ask if this is a second or, heaven forbid, a third
roof over the original. An easy way to detect if the roof you are viewing is a second roof is to stand back at a far enough distance so that a
slight shadow is cast over part of the roof. If it is a second roof, the
center of each **shingle tab** will show a slight depression or cupping.
(Expansion from a roof under a roof will cause great distortion.) The
tabs of a shingle roof should appear flat.

For a roll asphalt composition roofing the same consideration
should be applied as for the shingles. A house with roll roofing should
be viewed as a liability because of all kinds of roofing it is most easily
damaged. You will find this type of roofing on lesser-priced homes.

If the roof is covered with any of the other types of materials, an
experienced roofer should determine its worthiness. Besides, it may be
dangerous to climb on these other kinds of roofs — they can also be
too steep for you or anyone else's safety. Even the most experienced
roofers tread very warily on steep roofs. If the house is located in the
snowbelt, a winter inspection of the roof can only be accomplished
when it is free from an accumulation of snow and/or ice.

Before you leave the roof, you will want to consider the chimney or
flue. For houses more than twenty years old, the mortar holding the
bricks or stone together may need **tuck-pointing.** Done properly, this
is a job that will cost in excess of $250. It's an expensive job because
of the height, and because a platform for working on must be constructed before the work begins on the flue.

For best protection the flue should be covered by a **rain shield.** It is
important for the rain shield to have a wire mesh **bird protector**
around it. This keeps birds from roosting under it, especially in cold
weather. These shields, depending on size, cost in excess of $50. In
addition to the cost of the shield there will be the labor necessary to
install it.

Unless you are actually on the roof, you will not be able to see
cracks and splits in the roofing, **valleys,** and deterioration of joints
around vents, the chimney, and **dormers.** Some roofs are too steep
for you to climb on. Should this be the case, use the life expectancy
formula for the roofing, coupled with its appearance, as seen through
your binoculars, to make your judgment.

The **roof edge** is an area frequently overlooked. The leading board
under the roofing is subjected to an abnormal amount of weathering.

If it is protected (see illustration #21) with roof edging, accumulations of snow and ice in the guttering will not attack this leading edge of the **roof decking**. Roof decking boards that do not have this roof edging applied will generally be in poor condition. Sometimes this deterioration is so severe that the boards will not hold a nail. When a new roof is installed these bad boards should be replaced. A responsible roofer will insist upon their being replaced. The same situation applies to the gable ends.

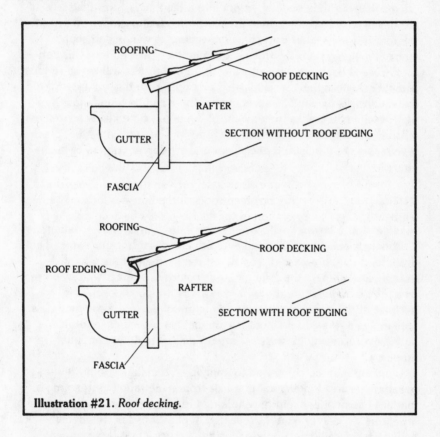

Illustration #21. *Roof decking.*

Guttering:

Is the guttering painted steel? Is it aluminum or is it plastic? Are the hangers or spikes anchored no more than 48″ apart? Are they loose? Is there enough pitch in the direction of the flow to the downspouts? Is the guttering covered with gutter guard? Do the seams and joints show evidence of leaks?

All of these are important questions. Answering in the negative can be reason to consider replacing the guttering. If replacement is necessary, consider continuous aluminum guttering. You would be safe to multiply the lineal footage by $4 which should include material and labor.

If the gutters are galvanized and painted, you can be sure that a repainting job will be necessary every five years or less depending on your patience with the unsightly appearance of peeling paint.

Downspouts should either empty into a tile that is connected to a storm sewer or have their own drain line directed to drain away from the house. Many times these tile connections run an underground course emptying onto the sidewalk or into the street gutter. This constant flow of large amounts of water from the gutters will cause serious ground erosion if the flow is allowed to empty onto the ground at the ends of the downspouts. Consequently, there can be foundation damage, resulting in cracks to the walls of the house both inside as well as outside. Be certain to look for these cracks. The application of **splash blocks** is a great help in reducing ground erosion at corners of the house.

Siding:

Is the house covered with wood, aluminum, vinyl, or steel siding? Is it a brick or stone home? You never have to paint brick or stone. That does not mean, however, that you are free of maintenance on it.

In all areas where the brick or stone comes in contact with wood or concrete, look for separations. These areas are points of stress because of the different molecular structure of each of these materials. Due to this stress a movement occurs that is imperceptible to the naked eye. Keeping these stress areas caulked requires continual attention.

Caulking may be compared to applying a bandage. Both are temporary measures to keep an area free from penetration by foreign matter. The bandage and the caulking are both temporary, but unlike the former, caulking requires repeated applications for an indefinite period. Some caulking is longer lasting, but none of it is permanent. The material itself may last a long time, but the area it is used on is constantly moving, thereby changing the configuration from its original shape. This is the reason for occasionally cleaning out the old and refilling the stress area.

Be *certain* to locate separations of brick or stone from the mortar. These would likely appear in a stair-step effect traveling up the wall from any given area, frequently at the corners of the house. This is

defect is only visual and will not need repair. To replace a dam-
panel requires a siding applicator or someone familiar with the
dure for removal and replacement of damaged panels. The cost
lace a single panel can cost $70 to several hundred dollars,
and material included. The cost will depend whether the dam-
area is on the ground level or on a higher level that requires
sion ladders.

e of the nice things about vinyl siding is its resiliency to hard
s. However, if the weather is very cold and vinyl is hit hard
gh, it can crack or shatter. Replacement of damaged vinyl panels
s complicated but as costly as aluminum. An additional advan-
of vinyl siding is that the color is homogeneous unlike aluminum,
is a painted surface. Scratches from abrasions on vinyl can be
d out; on aluminum siding a scratch must be touched up with
al paint.

el, like aluminum, has a painted surface. Like vinyl, steel can
tand shocks. The steel siding requires an electrical grounding
steel will easily conduct electricity. This grounding is necessary
because of the possibility of lightning striking the house.

th aluminum and steel siding require repainting. The length of
required between the initial application of the siding and its need
aint will vary depending on geographic location. The paint on
sidings should hold well for twenty to twenty-five years.

"chalking" effect on both steel and aluminum siding is a normal
nticipated occurrence. The paint "chalking off" is a way of main-
g a relatively fresh appearance, referred to in the industry as
hing." Some superior quality metal siding has a factory-applied
ng to reduce this "chalking." This factory coating is noticeable to
ye because the siding has a sheen, and maintains it longer than
ut the coating.

casionally you may view a house that has outside walls covered
stucco. Stucco is a mixture of Portland cement and sand. Water
ded to this mixture and applied with a trowel over a wire mesh
. This is similar to plaster on the inside of a house.

ouses that are stuccoed represent an era when labor was very
p. It was no small task to stucco a house. In parts of the country,
oed homes are common. If you are inspecting one, look for
us cracks. Deterioration also occurs at the bottom or leading edge
ot so much due to age as to having been struck with the lawn-
er handle, baseballs, and other hard objects. Many of these stuc-
houses present a better physical appearance than some wood-
houses.

u also may be inspecting a house that has been covered with
appears to be stone but is not. This is a man-made siding of

serious and may be an indication of footing failure,
directly attributable to erosion of the ground from d
downspouts. It may also indicate that an insufficient
ties were used at the time the masonry was laid. Th
of corrugated metal strap, ½" wide and 7" in length
on one end to the studs and imbedded in the mortar
They are all that hold the masonry to the building.

The seriousness of this defect can be the cause fo
inspection and turning down the house. On the othe
so interested in the house that this doesn't deter you,
the seller get a certified opinion from a structural en
the fact that this is not a serious problem.

If you are still interested in the house after learnin
serious structural defect, then negotiate with the selle
ponding reduction in the asking price in order to pay
correction.

A wood-sided house requires paint, unless the wo
redwood. Paint will not properly adhere to cedar or
of the oils inherent in the wood. It is not necessary to
cedar to keep it from deterioration. Staining will only
its appearance. If it is not treated, it will turn shades
Untreated redwood will form black streaks in the ag
weathering and not deterioration; the black streaks

Most wood siding requires painting and then repai
ten years. During that span of time there may be so
in greater need of repainting than others. This is cau
which is more prevalent around bathrooms, kitchens
ity areas. Most of the time the paint and its inability
surface of the wood takes the blame. Except in rare
fault is not in the paint. It makes little difference wha
exterior paint is used.

Moisture is constantly being drawn out of the hou
through the walls and insulation board and penetrati
ing. As it passes through, the moisture literally push
siding. If the paint looks very bad, it may point towa
unless painting a house is your "thing." Also the hou
inspecting may have just been painted and the paint
another several years at least. (Cost of a new paint
too much to estimate, depending on size, configurati
union labor, etc.)

Aluminum does not have the ability to withstand
objects such as baseballs, rocks, etc. Sometimes eve
or a windblown branch will dent it — and the dents

fiberglass material. It may be covering the entire house or only a portion of it. This siding is not the original but an application over other siding.

You may find yourself confronting a house that has been covered with asbestos. Asbestos siding became popular immediately following World War II due to the shortage of available wood siding. Where it still exists you will find serious defects. Two things will be evident: 1) some of the nails holding the siding to the wall will have disintegrated and 2) asbestos is brittle (it's the nature of the beast). Consequently you will find broken pieces in a number of places. This siding is no longer manufactured and replacement pieces are unobtainable.

Occasionally you may inspect a home that is covered with a composition soft siding of insulating fibers. It will appear mostly in brick form. If this type of siding has serious defects in it, re-siding with aluminum or vinyl should be considered.

Soffit and Fascia:

The **soffit** is commonly called the overhang or the eaves. The **fascia** is the ascending and descending finish board that is exposed on the vertical edge of the gables. Illustration #22 shows them both.

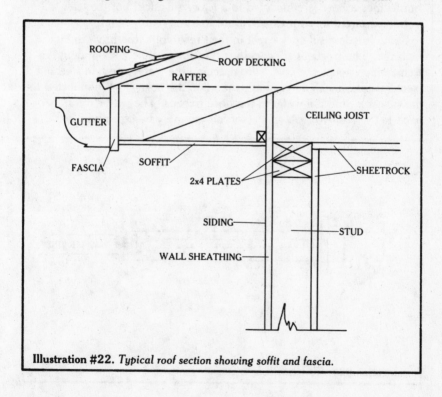

Illustration #22. *Typical roof section showing soffit and fascia.*

Look at these boards on the gable first. If they are not covered with aluminum, they will be a constant eyesore as the paint erodes. If they are covered with aluminum, hope that it was installed securely. Many aluminum fascia boards have had to be replaced due to faulty installation. Replacing a damaged aluminum fascia board will cost the $100 deductible amount of the homeowner's insurance policy and then some. This shouldn't be an arbitrary figure you allow for in your planning as long as it appears secure.

The paint on the soffit can show great deterioration. Covered with aluminum, the soffit can be very attractive, clean and maintenance-free. If it is not covered with aluminum, you should not consider it the seller's responsibility to cover it but something you may want to do after you own the house. Violent winds can damage practically everything. It especially takes its toll on poorly installed aluminum.

A soffit extending away from the house 20″ or more acts as a solar barrier in the summer. This keeps the sun from directly entering the windows most of the day. In the winter it acts as a buffer against the harsh winds and penetrating cold.

While you are walking around the house to check siding and soffit, take a look at the sill cocks, i.e., hose faucets. Manually operate each. Sometimes a hose is connected to a leaky sill cock, but the leak will not be apparent to you. Check it out to satisfy your mind.

Some frostless sill cocks split in their reservoirs and have to be replaced. The frostless sill cock has a reservoir tube surrounding the stem, which keeps the cold from reaching the water line and freezing it (see illustration #23). This happens when the hose is left connected to the sill cock, and the water in the hose freezes. The water will freeze back to the reservoir. A split reservoir can only be detected when the

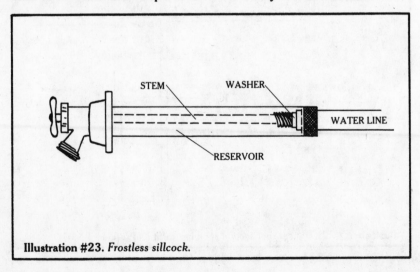

Illustration #23. *Frostless sillcock.*

water is turned on. This split generally isn't discovered until the first time it is turned on in the spring.

If you are inspecting this house in the wintertime, you will not be able to discover if such a split has occurred. It could be that the seller himself is not aware of this situation. Turn on the sill cock and if there is a split in the reservoir you will hear water spraying behind the wall where the split is located. Incidentally, before you do this, make certain that the connection isn't through a wall into a living area of the house; otherwise, you will cause damage to the wall and floor. Hearing that spraying water is the "alert" signal. Unfortunately the part that is split is on the other side of the wall and repairing it is out of the question — the sill cock will have to be replaced. The cost of replacing this will be approximately $100.

Windows:

You will now want to thoroughly check out the "eyes of the house," the windows. There was information given on windows while you were on the inside of the house, but not the outside. It is assumed that you have already looked at every window.

There are five common styles of windows: double-hung, casement, sliders, hopper, and awning. Occasionally you will encounter cottage and oriel style windows. (See illustration #24).

The double-hung is made up of two separate sashes that raise and lower vertically. The casement is a single sash that can be installed to crank vertically in or out. The slider is made up of two separate sashes, one stationary and one sliding, or two sashes that slide in either direction (similar to the double hung only these slide horizontally). The hopper is a single sash that tilts into the room. The awning type is a single sash that tilts out and up. Cottage windows have a taller top than bottom sash and are used more for aesthetics than anything else. The oriel window is the original name applied to the bay window.

The windows will appear much different to you from the outside. They will look cold and perhaps uninviting. The paint may have deteriorated. The caulking may be falling out or separated. Even the **glazing compound** (putty) holding the glass in place may be in a sad state of repair. Whatever you see, make notes on it. Remember to include in your notes any window that has broken or cracked glass.

You should inspect the appearance of all storm windows. The aluminum ones, because of age, may be badly pitted. This is not a defect; it is only unattractive. Some mitered corners on the frames may be broken or have pulled apart. Some also may have cracked glass in them. A sash sitting askew in the frame indicates that part of the frame, sash, or both is broken.

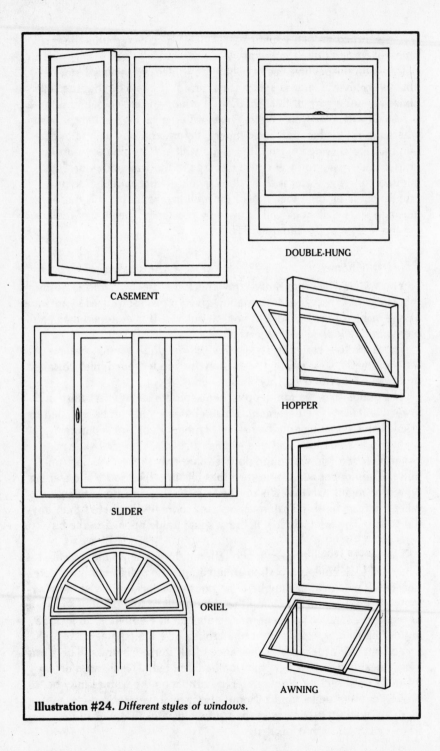

CASEMENT

DOUBLE-HUNG

SLIDER

HOPPER

ORIEL

AWNING

Illustration #24. *Different styles of windows.*

Whatever you see, make a note of it on the checklist furnished with this book. Take this information and prepare a repairs cost list. Assembling these costs will enable you to make an intelligent offer on the house.

Under the House:

A house with a crawl space will have an access door. Most are located outside the house. In some houses the access door will be inside of the house on the floor. An access door is the only way to get under the house for servicing water and drain lines, heating ducts, and other such mechanical necessities installed there.

In many parts of the country the main water shut-off valve is located under the house. This valve needs to be accessible. Crawling through a 32" wide by 16" high access door can be a difficult task for almost any homeowner. Sometimes one must crawl through snow, mud, or water to enter the access door and reach this valve. If this is the case for the house you are interested in purchasing, you should consider moving the valve into the house for easier access. The cost of moving the valve can easily run $125 or more if you hire a plumber. (The location of the main shut-off valve should not be a deterrent to purchasing the house. The owner is certainly not accountable for its placement.)

While you are under the house, look for loose plumbing pipes. If plumbing pipes are located close to the bottom edge of the floor joists and are not securely anchored, they will vibrate every time the water is turned off at any faucet. You may have already heard a thump or two as you turned off the faucets when you were inside operating them. With your hand, push upward gently on the water lines. If you notice a looseness, and the pipes are less than ½" from the bottom edge of the joists, you can be certain that the vibration caused by turning off a faucet will cause a thumping noise. It's nothing to be alarmed about, but the noise could become irritating, especially at night.

Vent doors (see illustration #25) are necessary to permit drying out of the floor in the crawl space. These vents are designed to be closed during the winter and opened during the summer. During the fall and spring rains the water table in the ground is at its peak, resulting in possible accumulation of amounts of water on the floor of the crawl space. Unless the vent doors are open through the summer, the water may not completely recede. Standing water is an invitation to vermin and becomes a breeding place for termites and silverfish. It will also produce mold and mildew on the floor joists.

If the clothes dryer has been vented under the house, there will be an accumulation of lint. You will want to correct this either before or

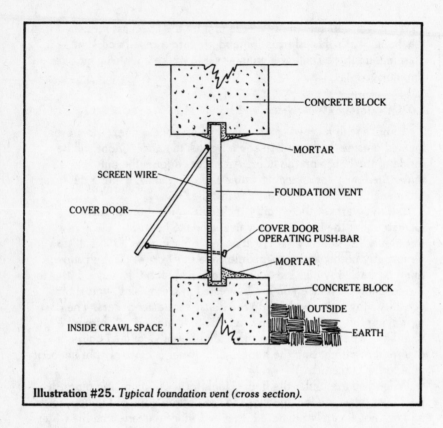

Illustration #25. *Typical foundation vent (cross section).*

shortly after you move into the house. It is permissible to vent the dryer through the floor but continue the run of the pipe through the foundation wall to the outside.

Porch and Stoop:

Whether the porch floor is constructed of wood or concrete, once it is painted it will require repainting. In older homes the porch might be in poor repair. Unless you look closely, you may not notice that the deterioration is substantial.

There is a way to determine how much value is left in a wood porch floor. Walk briskly the length of it several times to determine if you experience any bounce or vibration. Bounce is associated with deteriorating joists; vibration indicates looseness of boards. Both situations can exist simultaneously. Loose and rotting flooring boards will be cupped and do not hold paint very long. As you make a note about this look also for any deterioration of the front trim or **belt board.**

Unless it is seriously separating from the house, a concrete porch is a real gem. Separation is a problem that will increase as long as it is left unattended. While you are not likely to fall through it, the separation invites dirt, leaves, debris, and nests of small vermin. It is a definite eyesore.

This situation will be one you should insist upon correcting before or shortly after you move in. Make this one of your established priorities. Sometimes repairing a badly deteriorated porch is not possible. It may require removing it completely and/or rebuilding it. This is a major cost of several thousand dollars.

Look up to the ceiling of the porch. Are there watermarks indicative of leaks from the roof? Is the stain or paint peeling severely? This last item is another indication of moisture — a clue that moisture in the attic is trapped and has no place but the porch ceiling to dissipate. (Several or more louvers (6″ by 12″) strategically placed will permit the moisture to remove itself.)

Are the railings and support columns in solid condition? You may find rotting and crumbling at the base of many wood support columns. Make a note about it. The supports and the railing may be wrought iron. Check to see that the bolts anchoring them into the floor are not loose or rusted out.

Some support columns are brick or stone. When you find these, inspect their bases very closely. Wood or steel is easier to replace than masonry.

Stoops are small roof projections that are constructed mostly of wood, or occasionally of aluminum. These are built to protect an entrance door against rain and snow. Look for sagging where the stoop is pulling away from the house. If this is not noticeable to the eye, fully open the door. The door will rub against the ceiling of a sagging stoop.

While you are on the porch or at the stoop, check the storm door at each entrance. Do they close securely by themselves? Do the locks actually work? Do the doors drag the sill or bind in the frame as they are closing? Many times this drag is associated with loose hinges or an expansion of the sill. Check which it is. The former is easy to repair.

If the entrance door fits tightly in its frame and the storm door is properly installed, a vacuum will exist. This vacuum will not allow the storm door to close securely by itself when the entrance door is closed. The vacuum prevents the storm door closer from acting in its full capacity. A vacuum indicates that this entrance is ideally installed to minimize the penetration of cold air in the winter. To check this, slightly open the entrance door; then fully open the storm door and release it. If the storm door closer is properly functioning and the storm door is not in a bind, it should close easily.

Since you are at the entrances, it would be a good time for you to check the operation of the doorbell. You may have already done this. Such a little thing can be overlooked. If the bell isn't working, the solution may be as simple as replacing the button that operates it. The transformer may be faulty (highly unlikely). Some of the time a broken spring on one or more of the strikes is the cause for malfunctioning chimes. In this case the only solution is to replace the chimes. This will cost you only the price of the new one if you do it yourself; otherwise a repairperson may charge $100 or more.

Awnings:

Does the house have cloth or aluminum awnings? These can be a big help in the conservation of energy for any house. They keep the sun's hot summer rays from penetrating the windows for most of the day and much of the winter blasts from attacking these same windows. Keeping the ultraviolet rays from penetrating the windows also protects the drapes from fading, another plus.

Awnings, however, have some negative qualities. One is a snow load accumulation. In some geographic areas it is so severe that it can cause the bolts to come loose from the wall where they are anchored. Secondly, the ultraviolet rays of the sun do cause the paint to become dull, making repainting necessary. One other small thing is that wasps enjoy building nests in awnings. "Every rose has a thorn" is an ancient adage that will become more applicable as your inspection proceeds.

Although fabric awnings are not regarded as a plus, they are not necessarily a minus either. Properly maintained, fabric awnings will last a long time. The trouble with them is that they should be removed before winter and rehung in the springtime. If they are not removed before the snow season, deterioration from a snow load shortens their life considerably. Keep this in mind when you are inspecting a house with fabric awnings.

Outdoor Lighting:

Many houses do not have outdoor lighting. In recent years it has become a point of security. In some sections of the country where breaking and entering has become more prevalent, outdoor lighting is a must. With this type of lighting there is less likelihood of prowlers and other unwelcome strangers.

Houses that do not have any outdoor lighting should not be penalized. Consider lighting as something you will want to add. The cost to install outdoor security lighting can run from several hundred dollars to several thousand or more. A yard light operated with a switch at the entrance door inside the house can cost $600 or $700, including materials and labor.

Driveway and Walk:

Concrete can be a sore spot for many people. The concrete you are inspecting may be cracked in many spaces and in varying stages of buckling. Most people want to blame the concrete or the contractor who installed it. This is just not the case, however, in many instances. Even if the concrete had a proper base of sand or gravel, was reinforced, was of sufficient thickness, and was properly installed, it would still crack. Proper installation will reduce and restrict the amount of expansion, but the cracks will remain and continue to occur.

Some upheavals in sections of concrete are attributable to a lack of reinforcement. It is not necessary to become alarmed at this unless you find these defects very bad, such as in a patio off the rear of the house where the upheaval is causing water damage or door problems.

There is a good concrete crack sealant that is manufactured and used professionally in institutional and industrial applications. It costs about $20 a gallon and is available only in 5-gallon pails. You will find this at a masonry products supplier. It does not keep the concrete from cracking. The amount of elasticity inherent in this product keeps the crack filled for a much longer time than do less expensive, lesser quality products.

Outbuildings:

Do not let yourself become so lax at this point that you are willing to forego the inspection of the garage. If you feel that you cannot go another step, take a break. Get a cup of coffee or sit down and rest. Then you can start again. This is a worthy investment of your time. It will take this long and more to make a thorough inspection by a qualified house inspector. Included in his time would be a written report explaining all the points of his inspection. A good house inspector will most likely spend at least four or five hours in the investigation and the written report. If you can find one, he will charge you $40 to $75 an hour for a complete house inspection.

Back to the garage. Is it in general disrepair? What size is it? Is the garage door an overhead type? Is it constructed of steel or wood? Does it operate easily? Does it bind when traversing either direction?

Are there any broken glass panels? Are the wood section panels broken? Is the garage door steel? Is it bent or severely dented? Is there an **automatic door opener?**

An automatic door opener has several advantages. An opener performs a security function for the house. When the door is closed, it's impossible to manually open the door from the outside. That makes it burglar-proof. The other very important feature is that you needn't ever get out of your car to operate the door when you arrive home. In bad weather the door opener becomes a real friend. The garage without one cannot be penalized, but it is strongly recommended that you put one of these on your priority list for things to do later.

Maybe the garage door is the horizontal sliding type. Beware! These have not been installed in residences for a long time. This will indicate to you that you are at an older home before you even go inside the garage. Many of these doors still operate fairly well with a little maintenance attention paid them. At best, they require a bit of muscle to operate. Enter it on your list as a high-maintenance item.

A garage with either this type or swinging hinged doors will probably have been built with the sill plate and the studs close to the ground. Consequently, you might find rotting of this wood. Too many years and too much water have taken their toll.

Frequently the roof of a garage, unless it is attached to the house or is relatively new, will be in poor condition. Many times a garage roof leaks and the seller does not repair it. These older freestanding garages seen around the country were not originally housing expensive automobiles. When they do, the roofs are in good condition!

Other features you will be looking for in the garage are lights and electrical outlets. Older garages generally have simple wiring that is inadequate for today's needs. Generally there is only a single light in the center of the garage hung from a two-by-four and operated by a single switch in the garage only. Few older garages have an electrical receptacle. It is convenient when the garage is freestanding to be able to switch on the light of the garage from inside the house as well as from inside the garage. A two-way switch is required to perform that double switching function. If the garage is attached, you will have no need for this feature.

A plus for any garage is to have water and heat available. Many people use their garage as a woodworking workshop, for repairing the lawnmower, for changing the oil in their cars, for repairing a bicycle, and even as a place for playing ping-pong. Water and heat are a plus but not a necessity.

Does the siding of the garage match that of the house? If it doesn't but is in good repair and not unsightly, give it an O.K.

Perhaps there is a carport instead of a garage. Should this be the case, look for proper roof drainage and, in cold climates, the carport's ability to withstand heavy snow loads.

Today many carports are constructed entirely of aluminum. They have been engineered to maintain their shape. Unlike garages, carports make fine patios. They also require very little maintenance, especially if they are aluminum. Those that are attached are at their maximum strength and, if in good repair, are considered a plus.

An exception to this would be if the carport is so constructed that there is insufficient drainage away from the main roof. The joint where one roof is attached to the main roof can be a real troublemaker. A way to determine whether it is a problem is to climb up on its roof and look at where the carport is joined to the main roof. Large quantities of roofing cement spread on this joint as if in repeated applications are one indication of a problem. Another is concave depressions near or at the joint; these indicate that water is pooling. When you see these things, you may reasonably assume that there has been a water problem. The seller may or may not have cured it. Approach this situation, where one roof is joined to the main roof, with caution. Sometimes it is necessary to re-cover part of the main roof and all of the carport so that this joint is covered as one. You'll need to check this cost with a roofer.

Check any storage buildings, whether attached or freestanding. It is obvious that to be considered effective, these buildings must be free from moisture. Carefully look them over. You will find a place on the checklist to make a note about their condition.

Landscaping:

The landscaping at the house may be very beautiful or just the opposite. Here there is no middle ground. Either a person is intensely involved with the yard or not at all. The grass may be scrawny looking, which is an indication that the ground may be poor in nutrients, or that there has not been enough rain. What you may discover in this part of your inspection (which may have been your first step in looking over the house) is how interested the seller is in the outside appearance. Often this is a clue to what you might expect to find inside. Attractively presenting the grounds of any house is a laborious and not inexpensive investment. Sometimes a poorly attended yard is due to the health of the seller. A widowed person may have lost the desire for attending the grounds. Perhaps this is the most nebulous part of your inspection and should be viewed from that standpoint.

Trees are an asset to any house. You may find, especially in older neighborhoods, that the limbs need trimming. Some trees need trimming so badly that the limbs present a danger to the roof and the house. Another problem where large limbs protrude far over the roof is the enormous downpour of leaves in the fall. Even evergreens shed their needles each year. This fallout accumulates on the roof, especially in the valleys, and clogs the gutters and downspouts. An accumulation of leaf fall in the roof valleys causes rapid deterioration of the roofing below it. The accumulation should be removed before it becomes a problem.

PART THREE
EXTRAS

3 · EXTRAS

This chapter will cover "the other things." They are listed here for your ready reference: the water well pump, cistern, septic system, water softener, hub-end gate valve, burglar alarm system, intercom system, suspended ceiling tile, built-in vacuum system, built-in cabinetry, whole house cooling attic fan, microwave oven, trash compactor, humidifier, electronic air filter, stairway elevator, wood patio, second story outside stairs, fencing, glass sliding patio door, breezeway, gazebo, garden, swimming pool, hot tub, sauna, outdoor furniture, gas grill, and skylight.

Water Well Pump:

You may have no idea that the water supply for the house you are inspecting is furnished by a well. If it is not apparent, or on the real estate agent's listing, you should ask.

Some houses are supplied by both city water and well water. This occurs in houses that were built outside the areas originally supplied by the local water department. Subsequently, these areas have had water extended to them as the city limits expanded, and thus enjoy a dual water supply.

Having two water supplies can be cost-effective, allowing you to use the city water inside the house and well water for watering the lawn and garden, washing the car, etc.

Before you commit yourself to purchasing a house with a private water system, one very important part of your inspection should be considered. If the house you are considering purchasing is located near a chemical plant, heavy industry, farm fields that experience heavy use of chemical pesticides, roads that are heavily salted, or areas where salt is stored, make a stipulation in your offer to buy that a chemical analysis be made of the water supply.

Many water wells have variable degrees of concentrations of manganese and iron. These stain both plumbing fixtures and laundry. Other water wells contain additional amounts of sulfur, which is corrosive to pipes and to equipment it comes into contact with. Sulfur also has a putrid odor similar to that of rotten eggs.

The above explanations may be a good reason for you to install a water purification system in the house if you decide to buy it. However, the owner cannot be faulted for not having done this. It was not a priority for him.

If a water pump is the primary source of water supply to the house, you should be concerned with its age and its ability to deliver sufficient quantities of water when needed. Fortunately, the water pump is an item that people will not hesitate to keep in good working order.

If the well is the primary water source, turn on the faucet to check the intensity of the water flow. One simple way to do this is to let the water run for several minutes. If the pump is in good condition, and there is sufficient water, the drop in water pressure should not be severe. Water well pumps are designed to maintain a 40 to 50 p.s.i. (pounds per square inch) delivery flow. This pressure gauge acts similar to a furnace thermostat. Generally, the well motor will activate (cut in) as pressure lowers to 20 p.s.i, and it will cut out at 40 p.s.i. This is not as great as the city water pressure of 80 p.s.i., but it is sufficient.

Cistern:

Unless you are looking at a rural home, you will find that most cisterns have been filled in. In fact, you would be hard-pressed to find one inside the city limits of most cities today. They are undesirable because they breed mosquitoes and are a danger to curious children if not adequately sealed.

Briefly, cisterns are a way of storing water. They are constructed of brick or concrete and used as reservoirs. They need to be supplied by a hauler of water. They generally are a holdover from the past. But they are still in use in areas where city water is inaccessible and by those who prefer this to well water. The water is either carried by hand from the cistern to the house, as in olden days, or transferred via an electric pump.

Septic System:

A septic system (see illustration #26) is a sewage collection and disposal system. A storage tank is buried in the ground at least fifty feet away from the house and is used to collect the wastes that pass out through the sewage drains of the house. In addition a **field bed** (clay tile) of varying lengths (200' to 400') is also buried in the ground. This field bed is connected to the outlet of the tank and is de-signed to accept the liquid waste that passes through the top of the **septic tank**. The solid wastes remain in the tank and decompose by means of putrification.

However, both the tank and the field bed must be cleaned out occa-sionally. This is done by a professional who uses vacuum equipment to remove the build-up and accumulation in the tank. Be sure to ask the seller when this was last done. (A tip for keeping the bacteria active in the septic tank is to flush several small boxes of yeast twice a year down the toilet.)

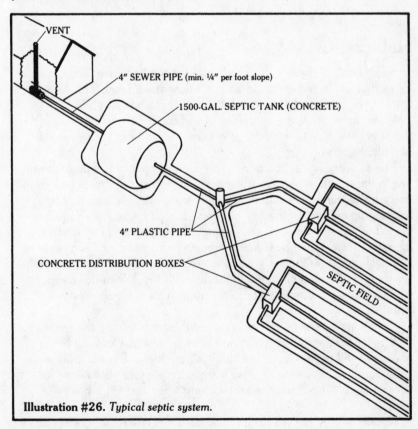

VENT

4" SEWER PIPE (min. ¼" per foot slope)

1500-GAL. SEPTIC TANK (CONCRETE)

4" PLASTIC PIPE

CONCRETE DISTRIBUTION BOXES

SEPTIC FIELD

Illustration #26. *Typical septic system.*

Water Softener:

A water softener is absolutely essential in houses where the water supply contains an abnormal amount of lime and iron. Heavy concentrations of these minerals can seriously damage water heaters, toilet flushing mechanisms, faucets, dishwashers, and laundry washing machines. White linens and clothing also suffer an unmistakable discoloration.

Water softeners are designed to reduce the amounts of mineral concentrations in the water. The cost of operation comes mainly from the salt that is used. In addition to asking the age of the softener, inquire about the quantity and cost of the salt used.

If you are concerned about the possibility of excessive concentrations of minerals in the water, there is something you can do. Take a small sample of the water to a local plumbing supply firm; they will test it for you. This will determine the level of mineral concentration and the need or lack of need for a water softener.

Hub-End Gate Valve:

Should one of these valves be located in the basement floor, it indicates that the basement floor is at or below street level. This hub-end gate valve has an important function. (See illustration #27).

When there are large quantities of surface water passing through the street sewer, and a blockage occurs, the water in the sewer will begin to back up.

The sanitary sewer line of a house is connected to this large sewer line in the street. When the street sewer becomes full and is unable to carry away the succeeding amounts of water pouring into it, a total backing up occurs. In the city all house sanitary sewer lines are connected to the street sewer. Depending on the amount of water filling the street sewer, the house line will begin to accept more and more of this back-up. If it reaches a valve to stop its backward flow, fine; otherwise it can back up into the bathtub and toilet. When this happens, it spills black liquid sewage onto the floor. This is a very nasty situation.

Only hand-operated valves are strong enough to stay the pressure that builds up during the rise of water in the sewer. Flooding of the basement will occur also if the valve is not closed. Because it is manually operated, it is wise to close it while away from your home for several days. Also it may require closing when there is a heavy rainfall.

Houses with crawl spaces or concrete slab construction rarely have

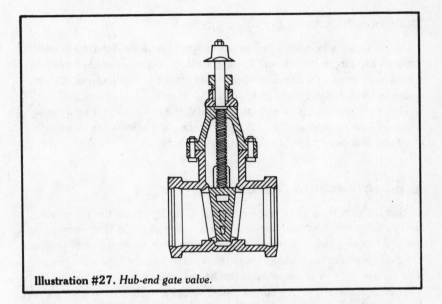

Illustration #27. *Hub-end gate valve.*

sanitary sewer stop valves in the line, whether they are at or below street level.

If you purchase a house that has the possibility of sewage water flooding into it, be sure to include surface water damage as a rider on your homeowner's insurance policy. The homeowner's policy will *not* have this *inclusion* unless you request it. The premium for this rider may be in the neighborhood of $35 annually. One such claim can easily amount to ten years of premiums.

Burglar Alarm System:

Where you find an alarm system it is safe to assume that it is in excellent condition. The owner might be reluctant to explain its operation to you until after you've purchased the house.

Intercom System:

It is not uncommon to find the intercom system inoperative or defective. Be certain to check out its operation. If there are monitoring stations in each of the bedrooms, you'll want to operate them to see if they work.

Properly operating systems can ease your mind if your family includes small children. Intercom stations also ease the burden of calling teenagers to answer the telephone. An intercom that has a station at the entrance doors enables you to find out who is knocking at your door before you open it, as well as saving you steps going there.

Suspended Ceiling Tile:

Many times suspended ceiling tile is found in older homes where the ceilings are ten to twelve feet in height off the floor. This tile has been installed to make the heating and cooling more cost-effective. It also hides defects in the ceiling plaster.

If the tile panels are of superior quality, they will have a vinyl coating that was applied at the factory. This coating allows for cleaning the face of them and is identifiable by its sheen.

Built-in Vacuum Systems:

Built-in vacuums have not been as well accepted on the market as was anticipated. Certainly there are a number of them that were installed as original equipment while the house was being constructed. Properly installed and maintained, they have two distinct advantages: 1) one has only to carry around the hose because the outlets for vacuuming are installed in the walls. It's just a matter of plugging the hose into them. 2) The noise of the motor is removed from "earshot." The motor and collection bag is either installed in the basement or the garage. The size of the dust receiver is much larger than with conventional vacuum sweepers. The filter at the receiver does need occasional cleaning.

If you notice that a receptacle for the vacuum does not have a cover plate, it is aesthetically distracting but not a real problem. Occasionally the cover plates get broken from being handled too roughly. It is a simple matter to replace the entire receptacle. In fact, it is similar to an electrical duplex receptacle because each of them is charged with electricity. The cost of a vacuum receptacle with the cover plate (the cover plate is hinged to it) is about $20. That is the cost of the material. A central vacuum system is to be considered an asset.

Built-in Cabinetry:

There's a wide variety of wood built-ins to be found in homes. What you should be looking for is faulty door and drawer operation, damaged hardware, severely damaged wood, and cracked glass. Even a wet bar should be checked out. Operate the faucet and drain the same way as you would at any other sink.

If you are a person who enjoys dusting, the more open shelving in these built-ins, the greater will be your joy. Glass doors covering the bookshelves will make housekeeping easier. Many shelves can be a real plus unless you would have difficulty filling them.

Whole House Cooling Attic Fan:

Attic fans generally are located in the ceiling of the central hall. They are quite large (36" by 36" or more) and, if in good repair, operate quietly.

Be certain to turn on the fan even if it is wintertime. If you are purchasing the house in the cold months, you might not learn of a problem until late spring. The problem would then be yours.

One problem might be a defective motor bearing. This would sound like metal hitting against metal. The sound is not unlike the "clacking" sound of railroad wheels turning on their tracks. That sound means that the motor needs to be repaired or replaced. The cost of this is in the neighborhood of $150.

Another sound you may hear will be loose slats flapping in the frame while the fan is operating. The slats may only require some lubricant, but it may be that one of the hinges is cracked on the end of a slat. If this is the case, nothing can be done to cure the problem except to replace the entire frame. Unless the noise is quite loud, in which case it shouldn't be operated at all, this defect is something most people can live with.

Microwave Oven:

Most microwave ovens and trash compactors are freestanding, and the seller will be removing them. If they are built in, determine the age of each. Remember you can learn the age from the metal identification plate.

Many microwave ovens carry a two-year warranty on the tube. Several manufacturers warrant their tubes for five years. Because the tube is the major repair item, you can do a little subtraction to determine just when the tube will probably need to be replaced.

Trash Compactor:

Trash compactors have been notorious for failure, requiring repeated servicing. Even if they are substantially warranted, frequent breakdowns can become a hassle. The cost of bags for trash compactors is an item to consider, especially in view of the fact that your grocery sacks come home with you at no additional cost.

Remember, it seems that manufacturers **plan obsolescence** of major electrical appliances. Therefore, be warned. Determine the age of every major appliance that you come in contact with during your inspection. Write each of them down on your checklist.

Humidifiers and Electronic Air Filters:

Humidifiers and electronic air filters are add-ons for natural-gas-fired, forced-air furnaces. The humidifier (see illustration #28) is an excellent way to maintain proper moisture content in the air throughout the house during the heating season. In the winter months the humidity levels are lower because cold air is drier than warm air. Gas heat dries the air circulating throughout the house. The drier the air, the more static electricity there is, the drier your skin becomes, the quicker the wood of the furniture starts to craze, etc. Consider a humidifier a definite plus.

You will be looking for heavy mineral deposits on the absorption pads or wheel. This will tell you how well the unit has been kept clean and what may be required of you after you move in. You should clean a humidifier each year. Replace the absorption pads or wheel while you are at it. The entire unit will quickly become ineffective without an annual cleaning. This small electrical add-on to the furnace will last a very long time, if it is cleaned thoroughly every year. A replacement for a furnace humidifer costs several hundred dollars.

An electronic air filter removes a substantial amount of dust and pollen from the circulated air in the house. If kept clean, it does a fine job. The electronic wires are critical to the effective operation of the unit. If one of these wires is broken, the unit becomes short-circuited and no longer functions.

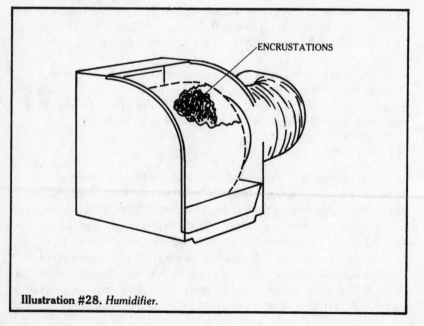

ENCRUSTATIONS

Illustration #28. *Humidifier.*

Replacing the wires is not a difficult or costly thing to do, and does not require a serviceman. The wires have T-shaped ends that hook into a slot on each side of the unit. These wires cost about $1.50 each. It would not be a bad idea to ask the seller how often he has to replace these wires.

Depending on the amount of lint and dust in the air, washing the unit several times a year will be all that is necessary. Replacing a broken wire occasionally and washing the unit is all the maintenance required.

Stairway Elevators:

On rare occasions you might look at a house that has a single-seat elevator. Most of the time it is attached to the steps and wall going to the basement. These are real step savers for invalids, the aged, and the not-so-young. An elevator allows a person to go in either direction with a load of clothes, laundry, a box, etc., while sitting on the elevator. This gives a freedom of movement that could otherwise be denied a disabled person.

The maintenance of this type elevator requires lubrication of the track and chain. A malfunction is rarely more than an interruption of electricity.

Now you can look at all the other things *outside* of the house.

Wood Patio:

Since 1980 wood patios have become a big item in some parts of the country (Midwest and Northeast). In the South and West they've been around for a long time. Wood patios come in every shape imaginable. Concern should be taken to inspect right angle joints. Some patios are built with untreated or inferior wood.

Look for rotting joints and large knots that are loose. Large knots are your best indication of inferior wood. These substantially reduce the strength and stability of a patio. You will find, however, that the vast majority of patios are built of pressure-treated lumber. Some of this lumber is guaranteed against rot for twenty-five years by the supplier. Learn the age of the patio and you can determine the lumber's life expectancy yourself. If the wood is guaranteed, you will have the basis for a legitimate complaint should it not last the guaranteed lifetime.

Second-Story Stairs:

When you are confronted with a second-story outside staircase in your inspection trip, view it the same way as you did the patio. Solid railings and post supports are important to everyone's safety. Make the appropriate note on your checklist for future reference.

Fencing:

Wood fencing is becoming very popular in some parts of the country. Fences range from good to absolutely useless. Many times the wood posts have rotted in the ground. This may not be perceptible to the untrained eye, but this book is going to help you learn what to look for.

Are you going to be able to detect most rotting posts by pushing on them? No! Do not push on them. You don't want to have a repair bill before you buy the house. The eye is very accurate in discerning level and plumb lines and should be able to tell that the fence is sitting askew or has some additional support indicating that it is unstable.

How else might you tell if the posts are rotted at the base? Rotted marks may be visible near the ground. Rotted posts show deep veins of soft grain loss and may show small holes of termite infestation. Many wood fence posts are not treated lumber, or they are the wrong species of wood to withstand infestation and rot.

Chain-link fencing, which has a remarkable lasting quality, is common. Unless chain-link fencing has been abused, it should be in relatively good condition.

Be certain, though, to note on your checklist what kind of construction the fence is. Calculate the length and height. While checking, don't overlook gates. A gate receives more use than the fence and may be the only weak part in it.

Glass Sliding Patio Door:

Glass sliding doors made of aluminum leave a great deal to be desired. Many are energy-inefficient. Depending on their distance from the ground level, they can become difficult to operate. The closer they are to the ground, the greater their subjection to expansion and contraction of the sill. The screens rarely do a good job. The bottom track is a constant catch-all for dirt, sand, mud, grass, etc. This causes the bottom rollers to erode, which in turn makes the door increasingly difficult to operate.

Open and close the door several times — the screen as well. If the problems just explained are not present, shout a big hooray! On the other hand, if there is serious difficulty in opening and closing the door, consider spending $1000 or more and changing it to an **atrium door**. This type of door is the same width (generally 6′) as the sliding glass door. One half of it is stationary like the aluminum door, however, and instead of the opening door sliding, it swings on hinges. This type of door is far more secure and most energy-efficient.

Breezeway:

Breezeways are a source of joy and contentment to many people. Most of the time these are the coolest places you'll find in the summer outside the air-conditioned house. An outdoor person will find a breezeway an advantage that far outweighs other defects. Inspect it as you would a porch — for a moisture-laden ceiling and a seriously cracked floor.

Gazebo:

A gazebo is a charming addition to any house. It will require painting maintenance, however, and wasps find them attractive for their nests. It isn't an easy task to paint a gazebo, and it takes a large amount of paint. But a gazebo may have been something you have been looking for in the house you purchase. Inspect it, though, for rotted wood, to determine its real worth.

Garden:

A garden can really cause the horticultural juices to flow for the outdoors-type person. Whether it's a flower or vegetable garden or both, it can be the difference between buying the house or not. A good vegetable garden might be worth a thousand dollars or more, depending on its size, to an avid gardener. The presence of a garden indicates that the owner is a person who cares. Gardening takes a lot of care.

Swimming Pool:

The swimming pool in the ground is subject to hydrostatic pressure just as is the foundation of a house (see page 7). The maintenance of a pool can be relatively small, but its neglect can quickly become very expensive. Not every person considers a pool at a home a plus. Some people regard a pool as a hazard. The presence of a swimming pool does increase the cost of the liability portion of your homeowner's insurance policy as well as the real estate taxes. On the other hand, it also increases your popularity.

Look for broken tile or cracked concrete if the pool is in the ground. A fiberglass liner has the greatest longevity and will be free from severe damage by hydrostatic pressure. If the house is located in a part of the country where the winters are severe, it is very important to cover the swimming pool during this time. Freezing water expands and will cause crazing of the fiberglass liner. It will also set up the possibility for serious damage. (There is a material made for repairing fiberglass crazing.)

Walk around the pool completely and check closely for defects in the concrete or tile apron. The apron is more likely to have damage than the pool.

Hot Tub and Sauna:

Many times a hot tub or sauna is placed outdoors in the back yard or garage. Until a person uses one, it might be considered a luxury.

There is, practically speaking, no maintenance to either except an occasional cleaning. The only other consideration is the pump or motor on the hot tub, which should give good service for at least ten years.

Outdoor Furniture and Gas Grills:

Outdoor furniture is generally left behind because it's either too bulky and costly to move or is in poor condition. Consider it neither a plus nor a minus. Lawn furniture shouldn't be something you are required to pay extra for unless you really do want it.

Gas grills permanently installed in the ground are generally considered an asset. Any owner who has one has probably used it enough that it should be considered paid for by him and not be sold as an extra with the real estate.

Skylight:

Skylights became popular in the West and Southwest. Now they are to be found in virtually every clime and section of the country.

Look for water damage on the ceiling surrounding the skylight. If you don't see evidence of any leaks, you have a quality skylight and installation.

Skylights give one a good feeling of being compatible with nature. You're bringing the good of the outdoors into the house with you. A good quality skylight is an asset, especially if it opens to allow the flow of fresh air.

CONCLUSION

CONCLUSION

I hope you have been able to give the house your blessing. However, you may be the first in a long line of prospective buyers to view it. Perhaps you are the only one to have seriously and thoroughly inspected it.

A perfect gem is hard to find. So too will be the house you buy. There is not a single house you can find that can pass without some poor marks, and that is to be expected. Some will fail miserably and these are the ones that you want to beware of.

This *does not* mean that you shouldn't buy the house just because it needs repairs. What it does mean is that you should take your checklist home with you, sit down with your spouse or partner, and discuss it. You will want to get a cost analysis on those items on your checklist that you have indicated need repair or replacing. From this analysis you will be better informed about the costs of repairing or replacing these items. Then you can make a firm offer at the price you are willing to pay — or you may decide that you would rather not purchase the house.

You cannot be blamed for being cautious and wise. In fact, if everyone who purchased a house were equally as wise, the prices of real estate would perhaps reflect the true cost rather than an imaginary one.

If you decide you are no longer interested in the house, quickly inform the real estate agent or the individual selling the house of your decision. This person has been patient and has spent several hours with you at this point. Extend this courtesy.

All of the things that you have noted on your checklist represent costs in dollars to you or the seller. You should separate those repairs that are necessary from those you merely desire, such as wallpaper or paint. In the mix of all this you will arrive at an intelligent price based upon fact, not supposition.

The dollar amount being asked for the house is just that. Rarely is the piece of real estate sold for the "asking price." Once you have made a firm offer you are protected by law as a claimant to the real estate for a period of time, which is set out in your proposal. If that time limit is exceeded and your proposal is not denied or countered by the seller, you will have legal rights to possession. It is an assumption of real estate law in many states that unless your offer is countered or refused in writing, your offer is accepted.

Make your proposal in writing to this effect: "If you will repair or replace this and this and that [be specific in your list of demands], we will buy your house at the price you are asking for it." You can go on to say in your proposal that only after these demands are satisfied will you accept the house.

You may prefer to determine the cost of these repairs and offer your proposal as a deduction from the asking price. Submit this in writing to the seller along with your list of items. This will show the seller that your offer is not an arbitrary figure. Give him good reasons to seriously consider your proposal. Unless you show good reasons to make a substantially lower offer to buy, your proposal may be quickly denied.

The longer a house is on the market, the more likely you will be able to purchase it at the figure you offer. As long as a buyer's market exists in real estate, the buyer has the upper hand.

It was indicated in the introduction to this book that the real estate appraiser determines what the asking price of the real estate should be. If you can obtain a copy of the appraisal, you will be able to decide whether you agree with it or not. When you go to other houses listed on the appraisal sheet and view them from the outside, you may easily see the fallacy in establishing the price of the house you are viewing. Although the disparity between appraising firms is supposed to be no greater than 5%, this is simply not so.

For your offer to be considered sincere and viable, you must include a reasonable amount of money as a show of good faith. The larger your deposit, the more sincere your offer will appear.

GLOSSARY

ABSTRACT OF TITLE. A document tracing the ownership of a particular piece of real estate from its original land grant through its successive owners. All transactions affecting the ownership such as encumbrances, whether they be deaths, mortgages, wills, taxes, etc., are included.

AMPERAGE. The strength of an electric current, measured in amperes.

APPURTENANCES. In law, such buildings, rights, and improvements that are situated on the real estate.

ATRIUM DOOR. This originally was the door that led to a central porch. It now is applied to the patio door. The door is similar to the sliding patio door in only one respect: they both have one fixed panel that is operable. Instead of the operable panel sliding horizontally, it is hinged and swings in or can be mounted to swing out.

AUTOMATIC DOOR OPENER. An electronic device used in conjunction with a garage door to facilitate its opening and closing.

BALL COCK. Part of the flushing mechanism in the toilet tank. Its purpose is to fill the tank with water after flushing has been accomplished and act as a stop valve to shut off the water once the tank is filled to its proper level.

BALUSTRADE. A set of balusters joined at the top with a rail and affixed to a wall or floor that is used as a protective enclosure at a stair landing.

BASKET STRAINER. Removable piece of equipment for the kitchen sink drain that permits closing the drain in order to fill the sink. It also is a protection against small objects falling down in and clogging the drain.

BELT BOARD. Board installed along the perimeter of a wooden porch immediately beneath the leading edge of the porch flooring, used to cover the joists.

BI-FOLD DOOR. One type of double doors that are hinged in the center, operating on a header track and floor pivot. These are activated by pulling on a handle centered in one of the doors to allow full access.

BIRD PROTECTOR. Wire mesh affixed to the supports of the rainshield whose purpose is to keep birds from roosting on the flue in the winter and nesting at other times.

BRIDGING. Metal or wood pieces that are anchored diagonally to and between the floor joists in the form of an "X" to stabilize them.

BUILDING CODE. Set of rules formulated by each municipal, state, and federal regulatory commission for the express purpose of protecting the life and limb of the public.

BY-PASS DOOR. Type of double doors that are hung by roller hardware from a header track and slide horizontally. These permit only 50% access.

CAULKING. Soft pliable material, similar in texture to putty, used to prevent the penetration of moisture and air.

CHECK VALVE. In-line valve that operates automatically in one direction only and allows fluid to pass through a hinged "door." It closes once the fluid stops its forward flow.

CIRCUIT BREAKER. Type of electric fuse used in an electric service box for the purpose of activating or deactivating an electric circuit. It is constructed with its own switch so it can re-establish the flow of electricity through the circuit when it has been interrupted. SEE FUSE.

CLOSET COLLAR. Part of the toilet assembly that is securely attached to the drain below the toilet and to the top of the floor. Its function is to hold the footed bolts that protrude through the holes on either side of the base of the toilet. It is sometimes referred to as the floor flange.

CORIAN™. A hard-surfaced, man-made material of various thicknesses and sizes, similar in appearance to quarried marble. It is used for kitchen and bath countertops, as well as for wall treatments in bath and shower areas.

CRAWL SPACE. Area beneath a house between the floor and the ground. Its depth varies, but there is usually a minimum height of 24″. It is one form of residential construction.

DAMPER. Movable plate in a fireplace that when open permits the fumes and smoke to be drawn through the flue to the outside. When closed it greatly reduces the amount of cold air penetration into the room.

DEADBOLT LOCK. Lock constructed of a steel cylinder that is not spring-loaded. A key must be used on one side and a turn button on the other to operate a single lock of this type. A double lock of this type requires the use of the same key on either side to operate it.

DEEP-SEAL FLOOR DRAIN. U-shaped trap drain attached to the sewer line that is installed in the floor of a basement. It is used to transmit water accumulations from various sources. In the trap portion there is a float ball. It acts as a pressure seal against a rubber gasket on the bottom of the opening in the trap to prevent sewage water backing up into the basement.

DISAPPEARING STAIRS. Folding set of stairs installed in the ceiling of a room to permit access to the area above the floor. It is most widely used as the access to an attic.

DORMER. Upright projection on a sloping roof. It also has its own roof and usually a window. The window provides light and ventilation to the area behind it.

ELECTRIC SERVICE PANEL. Box in which the outside electric power source enters the residence and is distributed through a set of fuses or circuit breakers.

ENCUMBRANCES. Legally, a claim (as a mortgage) against property.

FASCIA. Board that covers the soffit ends and leading edge of the gables of a house.

FIBERGLASS TUB SURROUND. Type of material used to re-cover the walls surrounding a bathtub. It comes in large sheets (56″ high, various widths and configurations) and in three, four, or five sections.

FIELD BED. Refers to the tile installed below grade that is connected to a septic tank and used as the area for liquid waste coming from the house. Usually it varies in length from 200 to 400 feet.

FLOOR JOISTS. Pieces of wood or metal used to span an area from one foundation wall to a pier or another wall. The sub and finish flooring are attached on top of the floor joists.

FLUE. Passageway or chimney through which the smoke and fumes of a fireplace travel.

FOOTING. Mass of concrete of various configurations and density poured in the ground for the purpose of supporting the outside walls of a building.

FOUNDATION. Supporting part of a wall, i.e., the base. Materials can be concrete, brick, or concrete blocks.

FUSE. Disposable contact used in an electric service panel that permits the flow of electricity through a circuit. It is constructed with a thin wire element for the purpose of deactivating a circuit when it is overloaded. The wire element is a safety factor, eliminating a burn through of the insulation on the circuit wire, which could cause a fire. SEE CIRCUIT BREAKER.

FUSED ELECTRIC SWITCH. Separate switches, installed at various places (kitchen sink, furnace, etc.) to protect motors from damage on overload.

GLAZING COMPOUND. Elastic and resilient-type material used to hold the pane of glass in a window sash. It also is referred to as window putty.

GRADE LEVEL. Smooth horizontal or sloping ground surface on which a structure is situated.

HOSE BIBB. Single faucet that is threaded on its discharge mouth. A hose is attached to it to transfer water to a particular destination.

HOUSE INSPECTOR. Person schooled or on-the-job trained in the areas of building materials, construction methods, plumbing, electrical, heating and cooling, and appliances, who examines an entire house for defects.

HYDROSTATIC PRESSURE. Standing water in the ground that becomes a force of pressure against any solid surface, vertical or horizontal.

LAZY SUSAN. Built-in revolving shelf or shelves usually located in the corner of kitchen cabinets. It permits full and easy access to storage.

LOCKING PLIERS. Tool with adjustable jaws, activated by a spring lever; when squeezed around an object, the jaws clamp shut. Also called Vise-Grips®.

LOUVER DOOR. Type of door of varying sizes that is partially filled with slats to allow for the passage of air.

MAIN WATER SHUT-OFF VALVE. Valve of varying sizes used to stop the flow of water from the water meter.

MECHANICAL. Catch-all term used in construction to designate plumbing, wiring, heating, and cooling.

MICA SURFACE. Refers to the mineral grains affixed to the side of the roofing that is exposed to the weather.

MOTOR BEARING. Friction-reducing machine part in which a shaft turns. It is used as a heat restrictor in a motor.

"O" RING. Rubber ring (or rings) of varying sizes used in faucets to allow easy operation and control of the leakage of water at various points.

O.G. (OGEE). A molding with an S-shaped profile. See illustration #29.

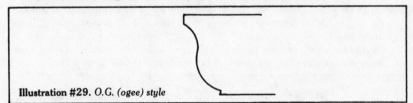

Illustration #29. *O.G. (ogee) style*

PLANNED OBSOLESCENCE. Phrase used to describe "apparent" terminal life of most major electrical appliances.

PLUMBING ACCESS DOOR. Small (generally 14″ x 24″) hole made in the wall at the drain end of the bathtub. Its purpose is to allow working room to service the tub drain and faucet.

POPLAR. Species of wood commonly used for residential construction during the eighteenth and early part of the nineteenth centuries. It was widely used because of its inherent stability and availability. Because of its texture, poplar was also used for finish trim and cabinetry. Some of the finer homes built in the South and Midwest can attribute their longevity to poplar.

POST FORM. Kitchen and bath countertops that are built of wood and covered with a plastic material formed with heat and roller dies to fit a particular configuration. See illustration #30.

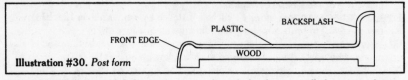

Illustration #30. *Post form*

PRESSURE RELIEF VALVE. Safety valve in residential plumbing installed on water heaters to allow the escape of excessive pressure build-up.

PRIME WINDOW. Window used in the original construction of a house.

RAFTER. Roof timber used to support the slope of a roof from its ridge to the wall of the building.

RAINSHIELD. Metal cap whose purpose is to greatly reduce the amount of water entering the flue. It is made to fit the size of the flue or its liner, set at 6″ to 8″ above the top of the flue, suspended by metal angles, and anchored by a metal band. Sometimes these angles are set in the cap mortar of the flue.

REPLACEMENT WINDOW. Window manufactured to replace the prime window. They are made of wood, vinyl, or aluminum.

RESPIRATOR. Device, such as gauze, used to cover the nose and mouth to protect the lungs from inhaling harmful substances.

ROMEX WIRE NUTS. Small internally threaded plastic caps that are used to manually secure and cover ends of exposed electric wires (active or inactive).

ROOF DECKING. Wooden material attached to the rafters under the roofing.

ROOF EDGE. Leading board, sometimes referred to as the "starter board," of the roof decking.

SANITARY SEWER. Drain line in a house through which waste matter (food and human) and water passes into a municipal sewer or its own septic system.

SASH BALANCE. Part of the window designed as a counterweight for the window sash, whose purpose is to support the weight of the sash and maintain it at any given height.

SCUTTLE HOLE. Small opening in a wall, floor, or ceiling that provides access to an area.

SEPTIC TANK. Tank made of concrete or fiberglass that is set below grade to collect the solid waste matter from the house, which subsequently putrifies and decomposes.

SHINGLE TAB. One of the three pieces in a shingle (asphalt composition roofing) of a three-in-one design that is exposed to the weather. See illustration #31.

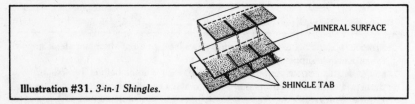

Illustration #31. *3-in-1 Shingles.*

SHORT CIRCUIT. Interruption of the flow of electricity in a given circuit.

SHOWER RECEPTOR. Floor or base of the shower attached to the drain.

SHUT-OFF VALVES. Valves installed at junctures immediately before faucets and toilets whose purpose is to turn off the water at these sources without shutting down the water supply for the entire house.

SILL COCK. Outside faucet to which the garden hose is attached.

SILL PLATE. Piece of wood (generally a 2″ by 8″) anchored to the perimeter of a residential foundation wall.

SINGLE LEVER FAUCET. Mixing type (hot and cold) faucet that has a one-control handle instead of dual handles.

SKYLIGHT. Metal and plastic unit, similar to a window, that is installed in the roof and permits natural light to penetrate the area. Some skylights can be opened and closed at will.

SOFFIT. Area of the roof that extends over the walls of a house. This is also referred to as the "overhang" or the "eaves."

SPLASH BLOCK. Concrete or fiberglass receptor laid on the ground at the openings of the downspouts to divert the water away from the house.

STEEL INSERT. Manufactured steel firebox intended to be used inside a previously built fireplace whose purpose is to produce more efficient heating than an open fireplace can. Because of its superior insulation, the steel insert can be installed as an independent fireplace unit and does not require a masonry surround.

STOP BOX. Water shut-off valve set 4–5 feet below the grade level and used to stop the flow of water between the municipal water line and the water meter.

STOP BOX KEY. Long T-shaped (6–7 foot) steel rod welded to a U-shaped foot and used to turn the stop box on or off.

STORM SEWER. Drain line not connected to the sanitary sewer system and designed to carry non-bacterial water.

STRIKE PLATE. Metal part of the lock that is anchored securely to the door frame and allows the door to be held in a closed position.

STUCCO. Mixture of sand and Portland cement applied over wire mesh that is attached to the wall of a house. It is used as an exterior wall covering instead of siding.

SUB-FLOOR. Wood (boards or plywood) that is attached to the floor joists and used as a base for the finish flooring.

SUMP PUMP. Water removal pump found in basements without a deep-seal floor drain and in crawl space-type homes that are situated in areas with a high water table level.

SUNBELT. Geographic area of the United States comprising the southern and southwestern states.

TEMPERED MASONITE. Material that is oil-impregnated and impermeable to water, readily available in sheets 48″ by 96″.

THERMAL BARRIER. Material placed between two metal window sashes to reduce the conduction of heat or cold. The purpose of the barrier is to reduce the amount of condensation that forms on the frames of metal windows.

TRANSFORMER. Device used to reduce the input of voltage for certain output sources, such as low voltage motors, doorbells, etc.

TRIP LEVER AND OVERFLOW. Unit installed on a bathtub that closes or opens the drain and also acts as a safety. Part of the unit has an opening around the faceplate installed several inches below the top of the tub, allowing water to escape, rather than accidentally overflow.

TUB FILLER SPOUT. Spout through which water flows to fill the bathtub.

TUCK-POINT. Process of partially removing old mortar from joints in masonry construction (bricks or concrete blocks), cleaning these joints, and applying new mortar to them.

TWO-WAY SWITCH. Switch that breaks the circuit at one station when deactivated and allows the circuit to remain open at the other station. These are commonly used in hallways, stairwells, and outbuildings.

UTILITY ROOM. Room designated for the placement and installation of mechanicals. **See MECHANICALS**.

VALLEY. Diagonal trough formed by joining two right-angle sections of roof. See illustration #32.

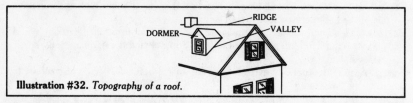

Illustration #32. *Topography of a roof.*

WALL TIES. Thin corrugated metal strips anchored to the wall and imbedded into the mortar of masonry whose purpose is to hold the veneered masonry to the wall.

WATER TABLE. Level of ground below which is saturated with water. The distance between the grade level (top of the ground) and saturation point varies in locales throughout the United States. The lower the sea level, the shorter the distance will be.

WEIGHTS AND CORDS. Very old method of sash balance for wooden windows. The weights are steel or cast iron cylinders of different sizes with a hole at the end of each one. A piece of rope (similar to clothesline cord, only stronger) of varying lengths to accommodate the different heights of sash, is tied to the hole. The rope is then threaded through a pulley installed in the vertical member of the window frame near the top. The rope continues downward and is attached to a plowed area in the edge of the wooden window sash. The sash travels vertically between wood stops in the frame and is held by the weights at any desired height.

WINDOW STOOL. A finish piece of molding (of various materials), cut and fit between the window frame, extending beyond the window casing. It is installed on top of the window sill inside the house.

WINDOW WELL. A corrugated steel water pressure breakfront. They are elliptical in design and installed immediately in front of basement windows. They reduce the water pressure against the wall below the basement window.

WINDOW WELL COVER. Translucent plastic material manufactured in an elliptical shape to conform to the size and shape of the window well and cover it.

WOOD MITER JOINT. A joint formed by the junction of two ends cut at equal angles, usually 45°. See illustration #33.

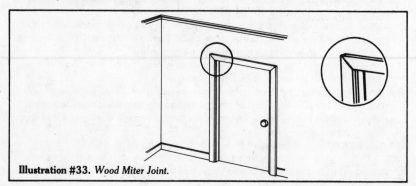

Illustration #33. *Wood Miter Joint.*

INDEX

CHECKLIST

Take the checklist that follows and inspect the house of your choice. You have been apprised of the many problem areas and what you should look for, as well as the things you should not overlook.

With this checklist you can identify those items in the house that you feel need repair or replacement and make a cost analysis. This analysis will enable you to arrive at a reasonable and realistic figure that you can state in your written offer to buy.

If it has been a while since you've read this book, I suggest you re-read it before you begin a serious inspection.

Ahead of you lies the wonderful world of "defective inspection." You may learn something about the construction and maintenance of a house. You may be surprised, after you have made a thorough inspection, to hear yourself say, "...there's a great deal more to a house than I ever realized."

CHECKLIST CONTENTS

Section One C-6

Basement ● Crawl Space ● Lower Level

Section Two C-10

Kitchen/Eating Area

Section Three C-14

Bathrooms

Section Four C-23

Bedrooms

Section Five C-30

Foyer ● Living Room ● Dining Room ● Family Room/Den ● Hall ● Fireplace ●
Stairway ● Stairway Elevator ● Security ● Patio Door ● Central Vacuum System ●
Skylight ● Attic

Section Six C-38

Garage ● Carport ● Breezeway/Solarium ● Porch ● Second Porch ● Outbuilding

Section Seven C-48

Entrances (Front, Side, Rear) ● Windows ● Sill Cocks

Section Eight C-51

Awnings ● Roof ● Guttering/Downspouts ● Fascia ● Soffit ● Siding ● Outdoor
Lighting ● Septic System ● Landscape ● Fencing ● Driveway ● Walks ● Wood
Patio ● Gas Grill ● Swimming Pool ● Hot Tub ● Sauna ● Outdoor Furniture/Play
Equipment ● Public Walks ● Curbs and Gutter ● Alley ● Other

CHECKLIST

Here you should enter the pertinent information about the real estate, which will be furnished by the real estate agent.

Address _____
Seller _____
Real Estate Agent _____
Tel. _____
Realty Firm _____
Tel. _____
Lot Size: _____ ft. W by _____ ft. D
Style of House _____
Sq. Ft. of House _____ ; Basement _____ ;
First Floor _____ ; Second Floor _____ ;
Age of House _____ Yrs. Taxes Per Yr. $ _____
Elem. School _____
H. S. _____
Distance to Municipal Bus _____
OTHER THINGS YOU WISH TO NOTE: _____
_____
_____
_____

You will want to rate the degree of apparent disrepair, or the lack of some items. For this reason the following rating is offered:

> **X** = Existent
> **O** = Nonexistent
> **A** = Satisfactory
> **B** = Needs Routine Attention
> **C** = Needs Special Attention
> **N/A** = Not Applicable
> A number (1, 2, 3, etc.) indicates the quantity

Example:

WINDOWS

(Mark number and condition of each) Double-hung __4__ ; Awn. __2__ ; Casement __2__ ;
Slider __1__ ; Jalousie _____ ; Wood __4__ ; Alum. __5__ ; Steel _____ ; Vinyl _____ ;
Lock __X__ ; Operable __X__ ; Paint __X__ ; Stain _____ ; Sill _____ ; Stool _____ ; Casing
_____ ; Glazing: Single _____ ; Double __X__ ; Triple _____ . Gen. app. __B__ .
NOTES: _Generally good_____
RECOMMENDED: _paint trim_____

You might prefer to use a rating system of your own making.

In addition to the rating spaces for each item, there are also spaces for other information, such as color, age, quantity, etc. Some spaces require a simple "X" or "O" to indicate the presence or lack of that item. All of this information is relevant to assist you with your cost analysis.

SECTION ONE

BASEMENT _____ **, CRAWL SPACE** _____ **, LOWER LEVEL** _____

Full _____ ; ¾ _____ ; ½ _____

Walls

Poured concrete _____ ; Brick _____ ; Concrete block _____ ; Cracked _____ ; Water-stained
_____ ; Gen. app. _____ ; Paint _____ ; Paneled _____ ; Other type _____ .
NOTES: _____
RECOMMENDED: _____

Floor

Dirt _____ ; Brick _____ ; Concrete _____ ; Cracked _____ ; Water-stained _____ ; Covered
w/carpet _____ ; Lino. _____ ; Paint _____ ; Tile _____ . Gen. app. _____ .
NOTES: _____
RECOMMENDED: _____

Basement Windows _____ ; Crawl Space Vents _____

(Mark quantity of each in appropriate blank)
Steel _____ ; Alum. _____ ; Wood _____ ; Painted _____ ; Rusty _____ ; Cracked glass
_____ ; Operable _____ ; Locks _____ ; Storm sash _____ ; Wood _____ ; Alum. _____ ;
Steel _____ ; Covered w/plastic _____ . Gen. app. _____ . NOTES: _____
_____
RECOMMENDED: _____

Basement Drain _____ ; Crawl Space Drain _____

Floor drain _____ ; Regular _____ ; Deep-seal type _____ ; Hub-end gate valve _____ ; Sump
pump _____ ; Filter lid _____ ; Float ball _____ ; Lint lid _____ ; Discharge pipe size _____ ;
Connected to _____ ; Noisy _____ ; Water drains quickly _____ . Gen. app. _____ .
NOTES: _____
RECOMMENDED: _____

Hub-End Gate Valve _____

Hand operated _____ ; Wheel operates easily _____ ; NOTES: _____
_____
RECOMMENDED: _____

Sump Pump _____

Submersible _____ ; Stand type _____ ; Check valve _____ ; Discharge pipe size _____ ; Drains
quickly _____ ; Noisy _____ ; Sump pit _____ ; Cover lid _____ . NOTES: _____
_____
RECOMMENDED: _____

Main Water Shut-Off Valve

Located in: Basement _____ ; Crawl space _____ ; Underground _____ ; Front yard _____ ;
House _____ ; Garage _____ ; Utility room _____ ; Meter pit _____ . Gen. app. _____ .
NOTES: _____
RECOMMENDED: _____

Water Lines

Steel _____ ; Copper _____ ; Plastic _____ ; **Located in:** Basement _____ ; Crawl space
_____ ; Underground _____ ; Overhead (attic) _____ . Anchored securely _____ ; Galvaniza-
tion _____ . Gen. app. _____ . NOTES: _____

RECOMMENDED: _____

Drain and Sewer Lines

Cast iron _____ ; Galv. steel _____ ; Copper _____ ; Plastic _____ . **Located in:** Basement
_____ ; Crawl space _____ ; Underground _____ . **Connected to:** City sewer _____ ; Septic
system _____ . Gen. app. _____ . NOTES: _____

RECOMMENDED: _____

Basement Stairs

Wood _____ ; Concrete _____ ; Steel _____ . Covered w/carpet _____ ; Tile _____ ; Lino.
_____ ; Paint _____ . Open _____ ; Enclosed _____ . **Handrail:** 1-side _____ ; Both sides
_____ . Securely anchored _____ . Low headroom _____ . **Light:** _____ W/switch _____ ;
Single pole _____ ; 2-way _____ ; Pull chain _____ ; At top of stairs _____ ; At bottom _____
; Fluorescent _____ ; Incandescent _____ NOTES: _____

RECOMMENDED: _____

Laundry Facilities _____
Washer Hook-Up

Located in: Basement _____ ; Garage _____ ; Utility room _____ ; House _____ . Water lines
anchored _____ ; Hose Bibs _____ ; 110 V outlet near _____ ; Anchored _____ ; Drain stand
pipe _____ . **Drains into:** Sump pit _____ ; Floor drain _____ ; Laundry tub _____ . Connected
to other drain pipe _____ . NOTES: _____

RECOMMENDED: _____

Dryer Hook-Up

Located in: Basement _____ ; Garage _____ ; Utility room _____ ; House _____ . Gas _____
w/shut-off _____ . Electric _____ 220 V Receptacle _____ . Securely anchored _____ ;
30A _____ ; 50A _____ , Vent line _____ . **Through:** Wall _____ ; Floor _____ ; Ceiling
_____ ; Roof _____ ; Into crawl space _____ . NOTES: _____

RECOMMENDED: _____

Basement Shower _____ (Not included in bath)

Metal stall _____ ; Fiberglass _____ ; Concrete block _____ ; Open _____ . Operable _____ ;
Anchored _____ ; Has door _____ ; Curtain _____ ; None _____ . **Drains into:** Sump pit
_____ ; Floor drain _____ ; Other drain _____ . **Faucet:** Single lever _____ ; Dual control
_____ ; Leaky _____ . Shower head _____ ; Hand held _____ ; Drain _____ . Gen. app.
_____ . NOTES: _____
_____

RECOMMENDED: _____

Basement Toilet _____ (Not included in bath)

Flush-up _____ ; Reg. _____ ; Pre-WW II _____ ; Shut-off valve _____ ; Age _____ ;
Cracked anywhere _____ . **Flush Mechanism** (handle, ball cock, tank ball): Operate _____ ;
Seconds to re-fill _____ . Secure to floor _____ . Gen. app. _____ . NOTES: _____

RECOMMENDED: _____

Water Heater

Brand _____ ; Size: _____ Gals. **Located in:** Basement _____ ; Garage _____ ; Utility room
_____ ; House _____ . **Gas** _____ ; With shut-off _____ ; Gas drip pipe _____ . **Elec.** _____ ;
Recovery rate _____ ; Gals. Per Hr. Relief valve _____ ; Discharge pipe _____ ; Run within 6"
of floor _____ . **Shut-off valve:** Cold _____ ; Hot _____ . **Condition of pipes:** In _____ ; Out
_____ . Vented properly _____ . Gen. app. _____ ; NOTES: _____

RECOMMENDED: _____

Main Electric Service Panel (Remove panel cover to inspect)

Brand _____ ; Size _____ Amp. **Located in:** Basement _____ ; Garage _____ ; Utility room
_____ ; House _____ . Fused _____ ; Circuit break _____ ; Qty. of circuits double-wired
_____ . **Type of wire:** Copper _____ ; Copper-clad _____ ; Alum. _____ ; Romex _____ ;
Greenfield _____ Spindle and knob _____ ; In conduit _____ . NOTES: _____

RECOMMENDED: _____

Water Well

Source: Primary _____ ; Secondary _____ ; Pump brand _____ . Age: _____ yrs. **Storage
tank location:** Basement _____ ; Garage _____ ; Utility room _____ ; Under house _____ ;
Outbuilding _____ . Self-Priming _____ ; P.S.I. **Operating pressure cuts:** in @ _____ ; out @
_____ ; Sufficient _____ ; Date last serviced _____ ; By _____ . NOTES: _____

RECOMMENDED: _____

Water Softener

Brand _____ ; Age _____ yrs; Active _____ ; Timer _____ . **Located in:** Basement _____ ;
Garage _____ ; Utility room _____ . NOTES: _____

RECOMMENDED: _____

Floor Joists

Size: 2 x 8 _____ ; 2 x 10 _____ ; 2 x 12 _____ ; Other _____ . **Gen. cond.** _____ .
Bridging: Metal _____ ; Wood _____ ; Anchored _____ . NOTES: _____
_____

RECOMMENDED: _____

Heating

Brand _____
Age: _____ yrs. **B.T.U.:** input _____ ; output _____ . **Located in:** Basement _____ ; Crawl
space _____ ; Garage _____ ; Utility room _____ ; House _____ . **Fuel:** Nat. gas _____ ; Oil
_____ ; L.P. gas _____ ; Elec. _____ ; Coal _____ ; Wood _____ ; Other _____ . **Type:** Hot
water _____ ; Steam _____ ; Forced air _____ ; Solar _____ ; Electric _____ ; Heat pump
_____ ; Floor _____ ; Wall _____ ; Room stove _____ ; Other _____ . Condition of vent
_____ ; Humidifier _____ . **Filter:** Electronic _____ ; Perm. _____ ; Disposable _____ ; Gen.
cond. _____ **Fuel bill:** NOTES: _____
_____

Ask to see the fuel bills for the two coldest months. Get an annual monthly average:
$ _____ .

Cooling

Compressor: Brand _____
Tons _____ . **Located outside on:** Concrete pad _____ ; Roof _____ ; Level _____ . **Date last
serviced:** _____ ; **By:** _____ . Separate elec. disconnect @ compressor _____ ; Gen. app.
_____ . NOTES: _____
_____

RECOMMENDED: _____
Ask to see the fuel bills for the two hottest months. Get an annual monthly average:
$ _____

Wood-Destroying Insects

To make this inspection you will need to use your screwdriver on both ends: the handle for sounding
and the blade for probing.
Areas inspected: _____
Areas obstructed or inaccessible: _____
For what reasons: _____
_____

Visible damage: _____
_____

Observed

Termite paths _____ ; Silverfish _____ ; Powder-post _____ ; Beetle holes _____ ; Mildew
_____ ; Fungi _____ ; Dry rot _____ ; Other _____
_____

Control measures evidence: _____ . **Date work performed:** _____ ; By: _____ .
NOTES: _____
RECOMMENDED: _____
N.B.: In addition to the above inspection for wood-destroying insects, also make a close inspection of
the structural soundness of the flooring, joists, drain, and water line under the immediate area of the
toilet. Note what you find: _____
_____
_____

SECTION TWO

KITCHEN/EATING AREA

Cabinets

Wood _____ ; Metal _____ . **Finish: Paint** _____ ; Stain _____ ; Plastic _____ . Base length
_____ ; In.; Wall length: _____ ; In.; Broken hardware _____ ; Gen. app. _____ .
NOTES: _____
RECOMMENDED: _____

Counter Top

Length: _____ In. **Post-form** _____ ; Backsplash _____ ; Formica _____ ; Wood _____ ;
Lino. _____ . **Corian** _____ ; Ceramic _____ ; Other _____ . Gen. app. _____ ;
NOTES: _____
RECOMMENDED: _____

Sink

Stainless steel _____ ; Porcelain _____ ; Cast iron _____ ; Single _____ ; Double _____ ;
Triple _____ . Anchored securely _____ ; Basket strainers hold water _____ . Gen. app. _____ .
NOTES: _____
RECOMMENDED: _____

Faucet

Brand _____ ; Dual control _____ ; Single lever _____ ; Dripping _____ ; Corrosion _____ ;
Spray attachment _____ ; Aerator _____ . Water purifier _____ ; Soap dispenser _____ ;
Insta-hot _____ ; Operable _____ . Gen. app. _____ . NOTES: _____
_____

RECOMMENDED: _____

Dishwasher

Brand _____ ; Age _____ yrs.; Model # _____ ; Operable _____ ; Noise level _____ ;
Separate shut-off _____ ; Drain connected _____ ; Disposal _____ ; Sink drain _____ .
NOTES: _____
RECOMMENDED: _____

Garbage Disposal

Brand _____ ; Model _____ ; Continuous feed _____ ; Batch feed _____ ; Operable _____ ;
Noise level _____ . NOTES: _____
_____

RECOMMENDED: _____

Separate Fuse Disconnect _____ ; (Located below sink in cabinet)

Dishwasher _____ ; Disposal _____ . NOTES: _____
_____

RECOMMENDED: _____

Refrigerator

W/real estate _____ ; Brand _____ ; Age: _____ yrs.; Color _____ ; Double door _____ ;
Single door _____ ; R.H. _____ ; L.H. _____ ; Model # _____ ; Self-defrost _____ ; Ice maker
_____ . Gen. app. _____ . NOTES: _____
_____
RECOMMENDED: _____

Cooking Top

Stove _____ ; W/real estate _____ ; Brand _____ . **Gas:** _____ ; W/shut-off _____ . **Electric**
_____ ; Receptacles securely anchored _____ ; Burners operate _____ ; Oven operates _____ ;
Broiler operates _____ ; Self-cleaning oven _____ . Gen. App. _____ . NOTES: _____
_____
RECOMMENDED: _____

Microwave

W/real estate _____ ; Brand _____ ; On a separate circuit _____ ; Operable _____ . Gen. app.
_____ . NOTES: _____
_____
RECOMMENDED: _____

Trash Compactor

W/real estate _____ ; Brand _____ ; Operable _____ . NOTES: _____
_____
RECOMMENDED: _____

Cooking Exhaust

Brand _____ ; W/light _____ ; 2-speed _____ ; 3-speed _____ ; Noise level _____ . **Located**
in: Ceiling _____ ; Cabinet _____ ; Wall _____ . **Vented through:** Roof _____ ; Floor _____ ;
Wall _____ ; Into attic _____ . NOTES: _____
_____
RECOMMENDED: _____

Drain

Steel _____ ; Copper _____ ; Plastic _____ ; Leaky _____ ; Sluggish _____ ; Gen. app.
_____ . NOTES: _____
_____
RECOMMENDED: _____

Water Lines

Steel _____ ; Copper _____ ; Plastic _____ . **W/shut-off** _____ ; Hot _____ ; Cold _____ ;
Separate shut-off for dishwasher _____ . Leaky _____ ; Corrosion _____ . Gen. app. _____ .
NOTES: _____
RECOMMENDED: _____

Light over Sink

Recessed _____ ; Surface _____ ; Incandescent _____ ; Fluorescent _____ ; W/wall switch
_____ ; Single _____ ; 2-way _____ ; Pull chain _____ . Gen. app. _____ .
NOTES: _____
RECOMMENDED: _____

Electric Receptacles

Number _____ ; Grounding type _____ . NOTES: _____

RECOMMENDED: _____

Ceiling Fixture

W/wall switch _____ ; Single _____ ; 2-way _____ ; Pull chain _____ . Gen. App. _____ .
NOTES: _____

Walls

Plaster _____ ; Sheetrock _____ ; Paneled _____ ; Paper _____ ; Wainscot _____ ; Paint
_____ ; Stain _____ . Gen. app. _____ . NOTES: _____

Ceiling

Plaster _____ ; Sheetrock _____ ; Tile _____ ; Paint _____ ; Paper _____ . Gen. app. _____ .
NOTES: _____

Windows

(Mark number of each) Double-hung _____ ; Awn. _____ ; Casement _____ ; Slider _____ ;
Jalousie _____ ; Wood _____ ; Alum. _____ ; Steel _____ ; Vinyl _____ ; Lock _____ ;
Operable _____ . Paint _____ ; Stain _____ ; Sill _____ ; Stool _____ ; Casing _____ .
Glazing: _____ ; Single _____ ; Double _____ ; Triple _____ . Gen. app. _____ .
NOTES: _____
RECOMMENDED: _____

Window Treatment

W/real estate _____ ; Drapes _____ ; Shutters _____ ; Blinds _____ ; Venetians _____ ;
Valance _____ . Gen. app. _____ . NOTES: _____

Ceiling Fan

W/real estate _____ ; W/lights _____ ; Operable _____ ; Sep. wall control _____ . Gen. app.
_____ . NOTES: _____

Floor Covering

Wood _____ ; Linoleum _____ ; Tile _____ ; Ceramic _____ ; Brick _____ ; Carpet _____ ;
Other _____ . Gen. app. _____ . NOTES: _____

RECOMMENDED: _____

Eat-in Area

Size _____ x _____ . Gen. app. _____ ; Telephone jack _____ ; Cable TV jack _____ .
NOTES: _____

Pantry

Walk-in _____ ; Built-in _____ . Gen. app. _____ . NOTES: _____

Special Built-Ins

(Enter sizes, finish, brand, and use) _____
_____
_____
_____
_____
_____
_____
_____
_____
_____
_____
_____
_____

Recommendations on All of Kitchen/Eat-in Area: _____
_____
_____
_____
_____
_____
_____
_____
_____
_____
_____
_____
_____
_____
_____
_____
_____
_____
_____

SECTION THREE

(THIS SECTION IS DEVOTED ENTIRELY TO BATHROOMS)

MASTER BATH

Casing and frame of door _____ ; Paint _____ ; Stain _____ . Gen. app. _____ .
NOTES: _____

Door

Hinged _____ ; Pocket _____ ; Folding _____ ; Paint _____ ; Stain _____ ; Privacy lock
_____ ; Operable _____ ; Close securely _____ ; In bind anywhere _____ . NOTES: _____
_____

Floor

Wood _____ ; Lino. _____ ; Tile _____ ; Concrete _____ ; Ceramic _____ ; Carpet _____ ;
Paint _____ ; Base _____ . Gen. app. _____ . NOTES: _____
_____

Walls

Plaster _____ ; Sheetrock _____ ; Paneling _____ ; Tile _____ ; Ceramic _____ ; Plastic
_____ ; Paint _____ ; Paper _____ ; Wainscot _____ . Gen. app. _____ . NOTES: _____
_____

Ceiling

Plaster _____ ; Sheetrock _____ ; Tile _____ ; Suspended _____ ; Stapled _____ ; Paint
_____ ; Paper _____ . Gen app. _____ . NOTES: _____
_____

Lights

Incandescent _____ ; Fluorescent _____ ; Ceiling _____ ; Wall _____ ; Swag _____ ; On
medicine cabinet _____ ; W/wall switch _____ ; Pull chain _____ ; Anchored _____ . Gen.
app. _____ . NOTES: _____
_____

Towel Bars

Number _____ ; Metal _____ ; Wood _____ ; Ceramic _____ ; Plastic _____ ; Other _____ .
Gen. app. _____ . NOTES: _____
_____

Exhaust Fan

W/timer switch _____ ; Switched w/light _____ ; Operable _____ . **Vented through: Ceiling**
_____ ; Wall _____ ; To outside _____ ; Into attic _____ . NOTES: _____
_____

Extra Heater

Located in: Ceiling _____ ; Wall _____ . Elec. _____ ; Gas _____ W/shut-off _____ ;
Operable _____ ; Condition of vent _____ . Gen. app. _____ . NOTES: _____
_____

Medicine Cabinet

W/lights _____ ; W/receptacle _____ ; Gen. app. _____ . NOTES: _____
_____

Electric Receptacles

Number _____ ; Grounding type _____ . NOTES: _____
_____

Bathtub

Steel _____ ; Porcelain _____ ; Plastic _____ ; On legs _____ ; Between end walls _____ ;
1-piece fiberglass tub and wall _____ . Gen. app. _____ . **Walls surrounding tub:** Tile _____ ;
Plastic _____ ; Ceramic _____ ; Other _____ ; Paneled _____ ; Paper _____ ; Paint _____ .
Plastic tub surround _____ ; Melamine board _____ ; Other _____ ; W/window _____ . Gen.
app. _____ . NOTES: _____
_____

RECOMMENDED: _____

The Faucet

Dual control _____ ; Single lever _____ ; Operable _____ ; Leaky _____ ; Brand _____ . Gen.
app. _____ . NOTES: _____
_____

Tub Filler

W/shower _____ ; Both operable _____ . Gen. app. _____ . NOTES: _____
_____

RECOMMENDED: _____

Tub Shower

Hand-held _____ ; Wall head _____ ; Water saver type _____ ; Loose _____ . Gen. app.
_____ . NOTES: _____
_____

Tub Drain

Trip lever and overflow: Operable _____ ; Leaky _____ ; Sluggish _____ . Gen. app. _____ .
NOTES: _____

Tub Enclosure

Sliding doors _____ ; Plastic _____ ; Glass _____ ; Curtain _____ . NOTES: _____
_____

Toilet

Wall hung _____ ; Low profile _____ ; Std. _____ ; Pre-WW II type _____ ; Age: _____ ;
yrs.; Shut-off valve _____ ; Operable _____ ; Cracked anywhere _____ ; Flushing mechanism
operable _____ ; Seconds to refill _____ ; Secure to floor _____ ; Floor surrounding toilet _____ .
Gen. app. _____ . NOTES: _____
_____

Separate Shower Stall

1-piece _____ ; 2-piece _____ ; 3-piece _____ ; Steel _____ ; Fiberglass _____ ; Built-in of ceramic tile _____ . Gen. app. _____ . NOTES: _____

Faucet: Dual control _____ ; Single lever _____ ; Operable _____ ; Brand: _____ ; Leaky _____ ; Corrosion _____ . **Receptor** (base): Fiberglass _____ ; Ceramic _____ ; Steel _____ ; Other _____ . Evidence of deterioration _____ . **Enclosure:** Hinged door _____ ; Glass _____ ; Plastic _____ ; Curtain _____ . Gen. app. _____ . Drain: Sluggish _____ . NOTES: _____

Lavatory

Metal _____ ; Plastic _____ ; Porcelain _____ ; Ceramic _____ ; Wall hung _____ ; Support legs _____ . Gen. app. _____ . NOTES: _____

Vanity

Size: _____ in. W x _____ In. D; Wood _____ ; Metal _____ ; Paint _____ ; Plastic _____ ; Stain _____ . Gen. app. _____ . **Top: Formica** _____ ; Marbelica _____ ; Ceramic _____ ; Plastic _____ . Gen. app. _____ . NOTES: _____

Drain: Sluggish _____ ; Leaky _____ ; Corrosion _____ ; Pop-up assembly _____ ; Operable _____ ; Pull chain and plug _____ . **Faucet:** Dual control _____ ; Single lever _____ ; Sep. hot and cold units _____ ; Leaking _____ ; Corrosion _____ . Gen. app. _____ . NOTES: ___

Water lines: Leaky _____ ; Corrosion _____ ; Steel _____ ; Copper _____ ; Plastic _____ . Shut-off valves: Hot _____ ; Cold _____ ; Operable _____ . NOTES: _____

Windows

(Mark number of each). Double-hung _____ ; Awn. _____ ; Casement _____ ; Slider _____ ; Jalousie _____ ; Wood _____ ; Alum. _____ ; Steel _____ ; Vinyl _____ ; Lock _____ ; Operable _____ ; Paint _____ ; Stain _____ ; Sill _____ ; Stool _____ ; Casing _____ . **Glazing:** Single _____ ; Double _____ ; Triple _____ . Gen. app. _____ . NOTES: _____

RECOMMENDED: _____

Window Treatment

W/real estate _____ ; Drapes _____ ; Shutters _____ ; Blinds _____ ; Venetians _____ ; Valance _____ . Gen. app. _____ . NOTES: _____

Ceiling Fan

W/real estate _____ ; W/lights _____ ; Operable _____ ; Sep. wall control _____ . Gen. app. _____ . NOTES: _____

Bidet

Shut-off valve _____ ; Secure to floor _____ ; Floor surrounding _____ . Gen. app. _____ .
NOTES on all of bathroom: _____
Any special installations: (Make appropriate entries here)

_____

RECOMMENDED: _____

SECOND BATH

Casing and frame of door _____ ; Paint _____ ; Stain _____ . Gen. app. _____ .
NOTES: _____

Door

Hinged _____ ; Pocket _____ ; Folding _____ ; Paint _____ ; Stain _____ ; Privacy lock
_____ ; Operable _____ ; Close securely _____ ; In bind anywhere _____ . NOTES: _____

Floor

Wood _____ ; Lino. _____ ; Tile _____ ; Concrete _____ ; Ceramic _____ ; Carpet _____ ;
Paint _____ ; Base _____ . Gen. app. _____ . NOTES: _____

Walls

Plaster _____ ; Sheetrock _____ ; Paneling _____ ; Tile _____ ; Ceramic _____ ; Plastic
_____ ; Paint _____ ; Paper _____ ; Wainscot _____ . Gen. app. _____ . NOTES: _____

Ceiling

Plaster _____ ; Sheetrock _____ ; Tile _____ ; Suspended _____ ; Stapled _____ ; Paint
_____ ; Paper _____ . Gen. app. _____ . NOTES: _____

Lights

Incandescent _____ ; Fluorescent _____ ; Ceiling _____ ; Wall _____ ; Swag _____ ; On
medicine cabinet _____ ; W/wall switch _____ ; Pull chain _____ ; Anchored _____ . Gen.
app. _____ . NOTES: _____

Towel Bars

Number _____ ; Metal _____ ; Wood _____ ; Ceramic _____ ; Plastic _____ ; Other _____ .
Gen. app. _____ . NOTES: _____

Exhaust Fan

_____ ; Wall _____ ; To outside _____ ; Into attic _____ . Gen. app. _____ .
NOTES: _____

Extra Heater

Located in: Ceiling _____ ; Wall _____ . Elec. _____ ; Gas _____ ; W/shut-off _____ ;
Operable _____ ; Condition of vent _____ . Gen. app. _____ . NOTES: _____

Medicine Cabinet

W/lights _____ ; W/receptacle _____ . Gen. app. _____ . NOTES: _____

Electric Receptacles

Number _____ ; Grounding type _____ . NOTES: _____

Bathtub

Steel _____ ; Porcelain _____ ; Plastic _____ ; On legs _____ ; Between end walls _____ ;
1-piece fiberglass tub and wall _____ . Gen. app. _____ . **Walls surrounding tub:** Tile _____ ;
Plastic _____ ; Ceramic _____ ; Other _____ ; Paneled _____ ; Paper _____ ; Paint _____ ;
Plastic tub surround _____ ; Melamine board _____ ; Other _____ ; W/window _____ . Gen.
app. _____ . NOTES: _____

RECOMMENDED: _____

Tub Faucet

Dual control _____ ; Single lever _____ ; Operable _____ ; Leaky _____ ; Brand _____ . Gen.
app. _____ . NOTES: _____

Tub Filler

W/shower _____ ; Both operable _____ . Gen. app. _____ . NOTES: _____

Tub Shower

Hand-held _____ ; Wall head _____ ; Water saver type _____ ; Loose _____ . Gen. app.
_____ . NOTES: _____

Tub Drain

Trip lever and overflow: Operable _____ ; Leaky _____ ; Sluggish _____ . Gen. app. _____ .
NOTES: _____

Tub Enclosure

Sliding doors _____ ; Plastic _____ ; Glass _____ ; Curtain _____ . NOTES: _____

Toilet

Wall hung _____ ; Low profile _____ ; Std. _____ ; Pre-WW II type _____ ; Age: _____ yrs.;
Shut-off valve _____ ; Operable _____ ; Cracked anywhere _____ ; Flushing mechanism
operable _____ ; Seconds to refill _____ ; Secure to floor _____ ; Floor surrounding toilet _____ .
Gen. app. _____ . NOTES: _____

Separate Shower Stall

1-piece _____ ; 2-piece _____ ; 3-piece _____ ; Steel _____ ; Fiberglass _____ ; Built-in of ceramic tile _____ . Gen. app. _____ . NOTES: _____

Faucet: Dual control _____ ; Single lever _____ ; Operable _____ ; Brand: _____ ; Leaky _____ ; Corrosion _____ . **Receptor** (base): Fiberglass _____ ; Ceramic _____ ; Steel _____ ; Other _____ . Evidence of deterioration: _____ . **Enclosure:** Hinged door _____ ; Glass _____ ; Plastic _____ ; Curtain _____ . Gen. app. _____ . Drain: Sluggish _____ . NOTES: _____

Lavatory

Metal _____ ; Plastic _____ ; Porcelain _____ ; Ceramic _____ ; Wall hung _____ ; Support legs _____ . Gen. app. _____ . NOTES: _____

Vanity

Size; _____ in. W x _____ in. D; Wood _____ ; Metal _____ ; Paint _____ ; Plastic _____ ; Stain _____ . Gen. app. _____ . **Top:** Formica _____ ; Marbelica _____ ; Ceramic _____ ; Plastic _____ . Gen. app. _____ . NOTES: _____

Drain: Sluggish _____ ; Leaky _____ ; Corrosion _____ ; Pop-up assembly _____ ; Operable _____ ; Pull chain and plug _____ . **Faucet:** Dual control _____ ; Single lever _____ ; Sep. hot and cold units _____ ; Leaking _____ ; Corrosion _____ . Gen. app. _____ . NOTES: _____

Water lines: Leaky _____ ; Corrosion _____ ; Steel _____ ; Copper _____ ; Plastic _____ . **Shut-off valves:** Hot _____ ; Cold _____ ; Operable _____ . NOTES: _____

Windows

(Mark number of each). Double-hung _____ ; Awn. _____ ; Casement _____ ; Slider _____ ; Jalousie _____ ; Wood _____ ; Alum. _____ ; Steel _____ ; Vinyl _____ ; Lock _____ ; Operable _____ ; Paint _____ ; Stain _____ ; Sill _____ ; Stool _____ ; Casing _____ . **Glazing:** Single _____ ; Double _____ ; Triple _____ . Gen. app. _____ . NOTES: _____

RECOMMENDED: _____

Window Treatment

W/real estate _____ ; Drapes _____ ; Shutters _____ ; Blinds _____ ; Venetians _____ ; Valance _____ . Gen. app. _____ . NOTES: _____

Ceiling Fan

W/real estate _____ ; W/lights _____ ; Operable _____ ; Sep. wall control _____ . Gen. app. _____ . NOTES: _____

Bidet

Shut-off valve _____ ; Secure to floor _____ ; Floor surrounding _____ . Gen. app. _____ . Any special installations: (Make appropriate entries here)

RECOMMENDED: _____

THIRD BATH

Casing and frame of door _____ ; Paint _____ ; Stain _____ . Gen. app. _____ .
NOTES: _____

Door

Hinged _____ ; Pocket _____ ; Folding _____ ; Paint _____ ; Stain _____ ; Privacy lock
_____ ; Operable _____ ; Close securely _____ ; In bind anywhere _____ . NOTES: _____
_____

Floor

Wood _____ ; Lino. _____ ; Tile _____ ; Concrete _____ ; Ceramic _____ ; Carpet _____ ;
Paint _____ ; Base _____ . Gen. app. _____ . NOTES: _____

Walls

Plaster _____ ; Sheetrock _____ ; Paneling _____ ; Tile _____ ; Ceramic _____ ; Plastic
_____ ; Paint _____ ; Paper _____ ; Wainscot _____ . Gen. app. _____ . NOTES: _____
_____

Ceiling

Plaster _____ ; Sheetrock _____ ; Tile _____ ; Suspended _____ ; Stapled _____ ; Paint
_____ ; Paper _____ . Gen. app. _____ . NOTES: _____
_____

Lights

Incandescent _____ ; Fluorescent _____ ; Ceiling _____ ; Wall _____ ; Swag _____ ; On
medicine cabinet _____ ; W/wall switch _____ ; Pull chain _____ ; Anchored _____ . Gen.
app. _____ . NOTES: _____
_____

Towel Bars

Number _____ ; Metal _____ ; Wood _____ ; Ceramic _____ ; Plastic _____ ; Other _____ .
Gen. app. _____ . NOTES: _____
_____

Exhaust Fan

W/timer switch _____ ; Switched w/light _____ ; Operable _____ . **Vented through: Ceiling**
_____ ; Wall _____ ; To outside _____ ; Into attic _____ . NOTES: _____
_____

Extra Heater

Located in: Ceiling _____ ; Wall _____ ; Elec. _____ ; Gas _____ W/shut-off _____ ;
Operable _____ ; Condition of vent _____ . Gen. app. _____ . NOTES: _____
_____

Medicine Cabinet

W/lights _____ ; W/receptacle _____ . Gen. app. _____ . NOTES: _____
_____

Electric Receptacles

Number _____ ; Grounding type _____ . NOTES: _____

_____

Bathtub

Steel _____ ; Porcelain _____ ; Plastic _____ ; On legs _____ ; Between end walls _____ ;
1-piece fiberglass tub and wall _____ . Gen. app. _____ . **Walls surrounding tub:** Tile _____ ;
Plastic _____ ; Ceramic _____ ; Other _____ ; Paneled _____ ; Paper _____ ; Paint _____ .
Plastic tub surround _____ ; Melamine board _____ ; Other _____ ; W/window _____ . Gen.
app. _____ . NOTES: _____

RECOMMENDED: _____

Tub Faucet

Dual control _____ ; Single lever _____ ; Operable _____ ; Leaky _____ ; Brand _____ . Gen.
app. _____ . NOTES: _____

Tub Filler

W/shower _____ ; Both operable _____ . Gen. app. _____ . NOTES: _____

RECOMMENDED: _____

Tub Shower

Hand-held _____ ; Wall held _____ ; Water saver type _____ ; Loose _____ . Gen. app.
_____ . NOTES: _____

Tub Drain

Trip lever and overflow: Operable _____ ; Leaky _____ ; Sluggish _____ . Gen. app. _____ .
NOTES: _____

Tub Enclosure

Sliding doors _____ ; Plastic _____ ; Glass _____ ; Curtain _____ . NOTES: _____

_____

Toilet

Wall hung _____ ; Low profile _____ ; Std. _____ ; Pre-WW II type _____ ; Age: _____ ;
yrs.; Shut-off valve _____ ; Operable _____ ; Cracked anywhere _____ ; Flushing mechanism
operable _____ ; Seconds to refill _____ ; Secure to floor _____ ; Floor surrounding toilet _____ .
Gen. app. _____ / NOTES: _____

_____

Separate Shower Stall

1-piece _____ ; 2-piece _____ ; 3-piece _____ ; Steel _____ ; Fiberglass _____ ; Built-in of
ceramic tile _____ . Gen. app. _____ . NOTES: _____

_____

Faucet: Dual control _____ ; Single lever _____ ; Operable _____ ; Brand: _____ ; Leaky _____ ; Corrosion _____ . **Receptor** (base): Fiberglass _____ ; Ceramic _____ ; Steel _____ ; Other _____ . Evidence of deterioration _____ . **Enclosure:** Hinged door _____ ; Glass _____ ; Plastic _____ ; Curtain _____ . Gen. app. _____ . Drain: Sluggish _____ . NOTES: _____

Lavatory

Metal _____ ; Plastic _____ ; Porcelain _____ ; Ceramic _____ ; Wall hung _____ ; Support legs _____ . Gen. app. _____ . NOTES: _____

Vanity

Size _____ in. W x _____ in. D; Wood _____ ; Metal _____ ; Paint _____ ; Plastic _____ ; Stain _____ . Gen. app. _____ . **Top:** Formica _____ ; Marbelica _____ ; Ceramic _____ ; Plastic _____ . Gen. app. _____ . NOTES:_____

Drain: Sluggish _____ ; Leaky _____ ; Corrosion _____ ; Pop-up Assembly _____ ; Operable _____ ; Pull chain and plug _____ . **Faucet:** Dual control _____ ; Single lever _____ ; Sep. hot and cold units _____ ; Leaking _____ ; Corrosion _____ . Gen. app. _____ . NOTES: ___

Water lines: Leaky _____ ; Corrosion _____ ; Steel _____ ; Copper _____ ; Plastic _____ . **Shut-off valves:** Hot _____ ; Cold _____ ; Operable _____ . NOTES: _____

Windows

(Mark number of each). Double-hung _____ ; Awn. _____ ; Casement _____ ; Slider _____ ; Jalousie _____ ; Wood _____ ; Alum. _____ ; Steel _____ ; Vinyl _____ ; Lock _____ ; Operable _____ ; Paint _____ ; Stain _____ ; Sill _____ ; Stool _____ ; Casing _____ . **Glazing:** Single _____ ; Double _____ ; Triple _____ . Gen. app. _____ . NOTES: _____

RECOMMENDED: _____

Window Treatment

W/real estate _____ ; Drapes _____ ; Shutters _____ ; Blinds _____ ; Venetians _____ ; Valance _____ . Gen. app. _____ . NOTES: _____

Ceiling Fan

W/real estate _____ ; W/lights _____ ; Operable _____ ; Sep. wall control _____ . Gen. app. _____ . NOTES: _____

Bidet

Shut-off valve _____ ; Secure to floor _____ ; Floor surrounding _____ . Gen. app. _____ . Any special installations: (Make appropriate entries here)

RECOMMENDED: _____

SECTION FOUR

MASTER BEDROOM

Casing and frame of door _____ ; Wood _____ ; Paint _____ ; Stain _____ . Gen. app. _____ .
NOTES: _____

Door

Hinged _____ ; Pocket _____ ; Folding _____ ; Paint _____ ; Stain _____ ; Privacy lock
_____ ; Operable _____ ; Closes securely _____ ; In bind anywhere _____ . NOTES: _____
_____

Floor

Wood _____ ; Lino. _____ ; Tile _____ ; Concrete _____ ; Carpet _____ ; Paint _____ ;
Base _____ . Gen. app. _____ . NOTES: _____
_____

Walls

Plaster _____ ; Sheetrock _____ ; Paneling _____ ; Paint _____ ; Paper _____ . Gen. app.
_____ . NOTES: _____
_____

Ceiling

Plaster _____ ; Sheetrock _____ ; Tile _____ ; Suspended _____ ; Staple _____ ; Paint
_____ ; Paper _____ . Gen. app. _____ . NOTES: _____
_____

Lights

Incandescent _____ ; Fluorescent _____ ; Ceiling _____ ; Wall _____ ; Swag _____ ; Other
_____ . **W/wall switch** _____ ; Single pole _____ ; 2-way _____ . NOTES: _____
_____

Electric Receptacles

Number _____ ; Grounding type _____ ; Number switch-operated _____ . NOTES: _____
_____

Closet

Number _____ ; Size _____ in. W x _____ in. D (inside dimensions); **Number** shelves _____ ;
Hanging rods _____ . (Mark number and condition); Lighted _____ ; W/switch _____ ; W/pull
chain _____ . Gen. app. _____ . NOTES: _____
_____

Closet Doors

Hinged _____ ; By-pass _____ ; Bi-fold _____ ; Operable _____ ; Wood _____ ; Metal
_____ ; Painted _____ ; Stained _____ . Gen. app. _____ . NOTES: _____
_____

Windows

(Mark number of each). Double-hung _____ ; Awn. _____ ; Casement _____ ; Slider _____ ;
Jalousie _____ ; Wood _____ ; Alum. _____ ; Steel _____ ; Vinyl _____ ; Lock _____ ;
Operable _____ ; Paint _____ ; Stain _____ ; Sill _____ ; Stool _____ ; Casing _____ .
Glazing: Single _____ ; Double _____ ; Triple _____ . Gen. app. _____ . NOTES: _____

RECOMMENDED: _____

Window Treatment

W/real estate _____ ; Drapes _____ ; Shutters _____ ; Blinds _____ ; Venetians _____ ;
Valance _____ . Gen. app. _____ . NOTES: _____

Ceiling Fan

W/real estate _____ ; W/lights _____ ; Operable _____ ; Sep. wall control _____ . Gen. app.
_____ . NOTES: _____

SECOND BEDROOM

Casing and frame of door _____ ; Wood _____ ; Paint _____ ; Stain _____ . Gen. app. _____ .
NOTES: _____

Door

Hinged _____ ; Pocket _____ ; Folding _____ ; Paint _____ ; Stain _____ ; Privacy lock
_____ ; Operable _____ ; Closes securely _____ ; In bind anywhere _____ . NOTES: _____

Floor

Wood _____ ; Lino. _____ ; Tile _____ ; Concrete _____ ; Carpet _____ ; Paint _____ ;
Base _____ . Gen. app. _____ . NOTES: _____

Walls

Plaster _____ ; Sheetrock _____ ; Paneling _____ ; Paint _____ ; Paper _____ . Gen. app.
_____ . NOTES: _____

Ceiling

Plaster _____ ; Sheetrock _____ ; Tile _____ ; Suspended _____ ; Staple _____ ; Paint
_____ ; Paper _____ . Gen. app. _____ . NOTES: _____

Lights

Incandescent _____ ; Fluorescent _____ ; Ceiling _____ ; Wall _____ ; Swag _____ ; Other
_____ . W/wall switch _____ ; Single pole _____ ; 2-way _____ . NOTES: _____

Electric Receptacles

Number _____ ; Grounding type _____ ; Number switch-operated _____ . NOTES: _____
_____

Closet

Number: _____ ; Size: _____ in. W x _____ in. D (inside dimensions); Shelves _____ ;
Hanging rods _____ (Mark number and condition); Lighted _____ ; W/switch _____ ; W/pull
chain _____ . Gen. app. _____ . NOTES: _____
_____

Closet Doors

Hinged _____ ; By-pass _____ ; Bi-fold _____ ; Operable _____ ; Wood _____ ; Metal
_____ ; Painted _____ ; Stained _____ . Gen. app. _____ . NOTES: _____
_____

Windows

(Mark number of each). Double-hung _____ ; Awn. _____ ; Casement _____ ; Slider _____ ;
Jalousie _____ ; Wood _____ ; Alum. _____ ; Steel _____ ; Vinyl _____ ; Lock _____ ;
Operable _____ ; Paint _____ ; Stain _____ ; Sill _____ ; Stool _____ ; Casing _____ .
Glazing: Single _____ ; Double _____ ; Triple _____ . Gen. app. _____ . NOTES: _____
_____

RECOMMENDED: _____
_____

Window Treatment

W/real estate _____ ; Drapes _____ ; Shutters _____ ; Blinds _____ ; Venetians _____ ;
Valance _____ . Gen. app. _____ . NOTES: _____
_____

Ceiling Fan

W/real estate _____ ; W/lights _____ ; Operable _____ ; Sep. wall control _____ . Gen app.
_____ . NOTES: _____
_____

THIRD BEDROOM

Casing and frame of door _____ ; Wood _____ ; Paint _____ ; Stain _____ . Gen. app. _____ .
NOTES: _____
_____

Door

Hinged _____ ; Pocket _____ ; Folding _____ ; Paint _____ ; Stain _____ ; Privacy lock
_____ ; Operable _____ ; Closes securely _____ ; In bind anywhere _____ . NOTES: _____
_____

Floor

Wood _____ ; Lino. _____ ; Tile _____ ; Concrete _____ ; Carpet _____ ; Paint _____ ;
Base _____ . Gen. app. _____ . NOTES: _____
_____

Walls

Plaster _____ ; Sheetrock _____ ; Paneling _____ ; Paint _____ ; Paper _____ . Gen. app. _____ . NOTES: _____

Ceiling

Plaster _____ ; Sheetrock _____ ; Tile _____ ; Suspended _____ ; Staple _____ ; Paint _____ ; Paper _____ . Gen. app. _____ . NOTES: _____

Lights

Incandescent _____ ; Fluorescent _____ ; Ceiling _____ ; Wall _____ ; Swag _____ ; Other _____ . **W/wall switch** _____ ; Single pole _____ ; 2-way _____ . NOTES: _____

Electric Receptacles

Number _____ ; Grounding type _____ ; Number switch-operated _____ . NOTES: _____

Closet

Number: _____ ; Size: _____ in. W x _____ in. D (inside dimensions); Shelves _____ ; Hanging rods _____ (Mark number and condition); Lighted _____ ; W/switch _____ ; W/pull chain _____ . Gen. app. _____ . NOTES: _____

Closet Doors

Hinged _____ ; By-pass _____ ; Bi-fold _____ ; Operable _____ ; Wood _____ ; Metal _____ ; Painted _____ ; Stained _____ . Gen. app. _____ . NOTES: _____

Windows

(Mark number of each). Double-hung _____ ; Awn. _____ ; Casement _____ ; Slider _____ ; Jalouise _____ ; Wood _____ ; Alum. _____ ; Steel _____ ; Vinyl _____ ; Lock _____ ; Operable _____ ; Paint _____ ; Stain _____ ; Sill _____ ; Stool _____ ; Casing _____ . **Glazing:** Single _____ ; Double _____ ; Triple _____ . Gen. app. _____ . NOTES: _____

RECOMMENDED: _____

Window Treatment

W/real estate _____ ; Drapes _____ ; Shutters _____ ; Blinds _____ ; Venetians _____ ; Valance _____ . Gen. app. _____ . NOTES: _____

Ceiling Fan

W/real estate _____ ; W/lights _____ ; Operable _____ ; Sep. wall control _____ . Gen. app. _____ . NOTES: _____

FOURTH BEDROOM

Casing and frame of door _____ ; Wood _____ ; Paint _____ ; Stain _____ . Gen. app. _____ .
NOTES: _____

Door

Hinged _____ ; Pocket _____ ; Folding _____ ; Paint _____ ; Stain _____ ; Privacy lock
_____ ; Operable _____ ; Closes securely _____ ; In bind anywhere _____ . NOTES: _____
_____

Floor

Wood _____ ; Lino. _____ ; Tile _____ ; Concrete _____ ; Carpet _____ ; Paint _____ ;
Base _____ . Gen. app. _____ . NOTES: _____
_____

Walls

Plaster _____ ; Sheetrock _____ ; Paneling _____ ; Paint _____ ; Paper _____ . Gen. app.
_____ . NOTES: _____
_____

Ceiling

Plaster _____ ; Sheetrock _____ ; Tile _____ ; Suspended _____ ; Staple _____ ; Paint
_____ ; Paper _____ . Gen. app. _____ . NOTES: _____
_____

Lights

Incandescent _____ ; Fluorescent _____ ; Ceiling _____ ; Wall _____ ; Swag _____ ; Other
_____ . **W/wall switch** _____ ; Single pole _____ ; 2-way _____ . NOTES: _____
_____

Electric Receptacles

Number _____ ; Grounding type _____ ; Number switch-operated _____ . NOTES: _____
_____

Closet

Number: _____ ; Size: _____ in. W x _____ in. D (inside dimensions); Shelves _____ ;
Hanging rods _____ (Mark number and condition); Lighted _____ ; W/switch _____ ; W/pull
chain _____ . Gen. app. _____ . NOTES: _____
_____

Closet Doors

Hinged _____ ; By-pass _____ ; Bi-fold _____ ; Operable _____ ; Wood _____ ; Metal
_____ ; Painted _____ ; Stained _____ . Gen. app. _____ . NOTES: _____
_____

Windows

(Mark number of each). Double-hung _____ ; Awn. _____ ; Casement _____ ; Slider _____ ;
Jalousie _____ ; Wood _____ ; Alum. _____ ; Steel _____ ; Vinyl _____ ; Lock _____ ;
Operable _____ ; Paint _____ ; Stain _____ ; Sill _____ ; Stool _____ ; Casing _____ .
Glazing: Single _____ ; Double _____ ; Triple _____ . Gen. app. _____ . NOTES: _____

RECOMMENDED: _____

Window Treatment

W/real estate _____ ; Drapes _____ ; Shutters _____ ; Blinds _____ ; Venetians _____ ;
Valance _____ . Gen. app. _____ . NOTES: _____

Ceiling Fan

W/real estate _____ ; W/lights _____ ; Operable _____ ; Sep. wall control _____ . Gen. app.
_____ . NOTES: _____

FIFTH BEDROOM

Casing and frame of door _____ ; Wood _____ ; Paint _____ ; Stain _____ . Gen. app. _____ .
NOTES: _____

Door

Hinged _____ ; Pocket _____ ; Folding _____ ; Paint _____ ; Stain _____ ; Privacy lock
_____ ; Operable _____ ; Closes securely _____ ; In bind anywhere _____ . NOTES: _____

Floor

Wood _____ ; Lino. _____ ; Tile _____ ; Concrete _____ ; Carpet _____ ; Paint _____ ;
Base _____ . Gen. app. _____ . NOTES: _____

Walls

Plaster _____ ; Sheetrock _____ ; Paneling _____ ; Paint _____ ; Paper _____ . Gen. app.
_____ . NOTES: _____

Ceiling

Plaster _____ ; Sheetrock _____ ; Tile _____ ; Suspended _____ ; Staple _____ ; Paint
_____ ; Paper _____ . Gen. app. _____ . NOTES: _____

Lights

Incandescent _____ ; Fluorescent _____ ; Ceiling _____ ; Wall _____ ; Swag _____ ; Other
_____ . **W/wall switch** _____ ; Single pole _____ ; 2-way _____ . NOTES: _____

Electric Receptacles

Number _____ ; Grounding type _____ ; Number switch-operated _____ . NOTES: _____

Closet

Number: _____ ; Size: _____ in. W x _____ in. D (inside dimensions); Shelves _____ ;
Hanging rods _____ (Mark number and condition); Lighted _____ ; W/switch _____ ; W/pull
chain _____ . Gen. app. _____ . NOTES: _____

Closet Doors

Hinged _____ ; By-pass _____ ; Bi-fold _____ ; Operable _____ ; Wood _____ ; Metal
_____ ; Painted _____ ; Stained _____ . Gen. app. _____ . NOTES: _____

Windows

(Mark number of each). Double-hung _____ ; Awn. _____ ; Casement _____ ; Slider _____ ;
Jalousie _____ ; Wood _____ ; Alum. _____ ; Steel _____ ; Vinyl _____ ; Lock _____ ;
Operable _____ ; Paint _____ ; Stain _____ ; Sill _____ ; Stool _____ ; Casing _____ .
Glazing: Single _____ ; Double _____ ; Triple _____ . Gen. app. _____ . NOTES: _____

RECOMMENDED: _____

Window Treatment

W/real estate _____ ; Drapes _____ ; Shutters _____ ; Blinds _____ ; Venetians _____ ;
Valance _____ . Gen. app. _____ . NOTES: _____

Ceiling Fan

W/real estate _____ ; W/lights _____ ; Operable _____ ; Sep. wall control _____ . Gen. app.
_____ . NOTES: _____

SECTION FIVE

FOYER

Floor

Wood _____ ; Lino. _____ ; Tile _____ ; Concrete _____ ; Carpet _____ ; Paint _____ ;
Base _____ . Gen. app. _____ . NOTES: _____
_____

Walls

Plaster _____ ; Sheetrock _____ ; Paneling _____ ; Paint _____ ; Paper _____ . Gen. app.
_____ . NOTES: _____
_____

Ceiling

Plaster _____ ; Sheetrock _____ ; Tile _____ ; Suspended _____ ; Staple _____ ; Paint
_____ ; Paper _____ . Gen. app. _____ . NOTES: _____
_____

Lights

Incandescent _____ ; Fluorescent _____ ; Ceiling _____ ; Wall _____ ; Swag _____ ; Other
_____ . W/wall switch _____ ; Single pole _____ ; 2-way _____ . NOTES: _____
_____

Electric Receptacles

Number _____ ; Grounding type _____ ; Number switch-operated _____ . NOTES: _____
_____

Closet

Number _____ ; Size: _____ in. W x _____ in. D (inside dimensions); Shelves _____ ;
Hanging rods _____ (Mark number and condition); Lighted _____ ; W/switch _____ ; W/pull
chain _____ . NOTES: _____
_____

Closet Doors

Hinged _____ ; By-pass _____ ; Bi-fold _____ ; Operable _____ ; Wood _____ ; Metal
_____ ; Painted _____ ; Stained _____ ; Gen. app. _____ . NOTES: _____
_____

LIVING ROOM

Floor

Wood _____ ; Lino. _____ ; Tile _____ ; Concrete _____ ; Carpet _____ ; Paint _____ ;
Base _____ . Gen. app. _____ . NOTES: _____
_____

Walls

Plaster _____ ; Sheetrock _____ ; Paneling _____ ; Paint _____ ; Paper _____ . Gen. app.
_____ . NOTES: _____
_____

Ceiling

Plaster _____ ; Sheetrock _____ ; Tile _____ ; Suspended _____ ; Staple _____ ; Paint
_____ ; Paper _____ . Gen. app. _____ . NOTES: _____
_____

Lights

Incandescent _____ ; Fluorescent _____ ; Ceiling _____ ; Wall _____ ; Swag _____ ; Other
_____ . W/wall switch _____ ; Single pole _____ ; 2-way _____ . NOTES: _____
_____

Electric Receptacles

Number _____ ; Grounding type _____ ; Number switch-operated _____ . NOTES: _____
_____

Windows

(Mark number and condition of each). Double-hung _____ ; Awn. _____ ; Casement _____ ;
Slider _____ ; Jalousie _____ ; Wood _____ ; Alum. _____ ; Steel _____ ; Vinyl _____ ;
Lock _____ ; Operable _____ ; Paint _____ ; Stain _____ ; Sill _____ ; Stool _____ ; Casing
_____ . Glazing: Single _____ ; Double _____ ; Triple _____ . Gen. app. _____ .
NOTES: _____
RECOMMENDED: _____

Window Treatment

W/real estate _____ ; Drapes _____ ; Shutters _____ ; Blinds _____ ; Venetians _____ ;
Valance _____ . Gen. app. _____ . NOTES: _____
_____

Ceiling Fan

W/real estate _____ ; W/lights _____ ; Operable _____ ; Sep. wall control _____ . Gen. app.
_____ . NOTES: _____
_____

Built-Ins

(Identify and comment) _____
_____
_____

General notes concerning living room: _____

_____
_____
_____
_____
_____
_____

DINING ROOM

Floor

Wood _____ ; Lino. _____ ; Tile _____ ; Concrete _____ ; Carpet _____ ; Paint _____ ;
Base _____ . Gen. app. _____ . NOTES: _____
_____

Walls

Plaster _____ ; Sheetrock _____ ; Paneling _____ ; Paint _____ ; Paper _____ . Gen. app.
_____ . NOTES: _____
_____

Ceiling

Plaster _____ ; Sheetrock _____ ; Tile _____ ; Suspended _____ ; Staple _____ ; Paint
_____ ; Paper _____ . Gen. app. _____ . NOTES: _____
_____

Lights

Incandescent _____ ; Fluorescent _____ ; Ceiling _____ ; Wall _____ ; Swag _____ ; Other
_____ . W/wall switch _____ ; Single pole _____ ; 2-way _____ . NOTES: _____
_____

Electric Receptacles

Number _____ ; Grounding type _____ ; Number switch-operated _____ . NOTES: _____
_____

Windows

(Mark number of each). Double-hung _____ ; Awn. _____ ; Casement _____ ; Slider _____ ;
Jalousie _____ ; Wood _____ ; Alum. _____ ; Steel _____ ; Vinyl _____ ; Lock _____ ;
Operable _____ ; Paint _____ ; Stain _____ ; Sill _____ ; Stool _____ ; Casing _____ .
Glazing: Single _____ ; Double _____ ; Triple _____ . Gen. app. _____ . NOTES: _____
_____

RECOMMENDED: _____
_____

Window Treatment

W/real estate _____ ; Drapes _____ ; Shutters _____ ; Blinds _____ ; Venetians _____ ;
Valance _____ . Gen. app. _____ . NOTES: _____
_____

Ceiling Fan

W/real estate _____ ; W/lights _____ ; Operable _____ ; Sep. wall control _____ . Gen. app.
_____ . NOTES: _____
_____

Built-Ins

(Identify and comment) _____
_____
_____
_____
_____

General notes concerning dining room: _____
_____
_____
_____

FAMILY ROOM/DEN

Floor

Wood _____ ; Lino. _____ ; Tile _____ ; Concrete _____ ; Carpet _____ ; Paint _____ ;
Base _____ . Gen. app. _____ . NOTES: _____
_____

Walls

Plaster _____ ; Sheetrock _____ ; Paneling _____ ; Paint _____ ; Paper _____ . Gen. app.
_____ . NOTES: _____
_____

Ceiling

Plaster _____ ; Sheetrock _____ ; Tile _____ ; Suspended _____ ; Staple _____ ; Paint
_____ ; Paper _____ . Gen. app. _____ . NOTES: _____
_____

Lights

Incandescent _____ ; Fluorescent _____ ; Ceiling _____ ; Wall _____ ; Swag _____ ; Other
_____ . W/wall switch _____ ; Single pole _____ ; 2-way _____ . NOTES: _____
_____

Electric Receptacles

Number _____ ; Grounding type _____ ; Number switch-operated _____ . NOTES: _____
_____

Windows

(Mark number of each). Double-hung _____ ; Awn. _____ ; Casement _____ ; Slider _____ ;
Jalousie _____ ; Wood _____ ; Alum. ___.___ ; Steel _____ ; Vinyl _____ ; Lock _____ ;
Operable _____ ; Paint _____ ; Stain _____ ; Sill _____ ; Stool _____ ; Casing _____ .
Glazing: Single _____ ; Double _____ ; Triple _____ . Gen. app. _____ . NOTES: _____
_____

RECOMMENDED: _____

Window Treatment

W/real estate _____ ; Drapes _____ ; Shutters _____ ; Blinds _____ ; Venetians _____ ;
Valance _____ . Gen. app. _____ . NOTES: _____
_____

Ceiling Fan

W/real estate _____ ; W/lights _____ ; Operable _____ ; Sep. wall control _____ . Gen. app.
_____ . NOTES: _____
_____

Built-ins

(Identify and comment) _____

_____

General Notes Concerning Family Room/Den: _____

_____

_____

HALL

Floor

Wood _____ ; Lino. _____ ; Tile _____ ; Concrete _____ ; Carpet _____ ; Paint _____ ;
Base _____ . Gen. app. _____ . NOTES: _____

Walls

Plaster _____ ; Sheetrock _____ ; Paneling _____ ; Paint _____ ; Paper _____ . Gen. app.
_____ . NOTES: _____

_____

Ceiling

Plaster _____ ; Sheetrock _____ ; Tile _____ ; Suspended _____ ; Staple _____ ; Paint
_____ ; Paper _____ . Gen. app. _____ . NOTES: _____

_____

Lights

Incandescent _____ ; Fluorescent _____ ; Ceiling _____ ; Wall _____ ; Swag _____ ; Other
_____ . W/wall switch _____ ; Single pole _____ ; 2-way _____ . NOTES: _____

_____

Electric Receptacles

Number _____ ; Grounding type _____ ; Number switch-operated _____ . NOTES: _____

_____

Closet

Number: _____ ; Size: _____ in. W x _____ in. D (inside dimensions); Shelves _____ ;
Hanging rods _____ (Mark number and condition); Lighted _____ ; W/switch _____ ; W/pull
chain _____ . NOTES: _____

_____

Closet Doors

Hinged _____ ; By-pass _____ ; Bi-fold _____ ; Operable _____ ; Wood _____ ; Metal
_____ ; Painted _____ ; Stained _____ . Gen. app. _____ . NOTES: _____

_____

Whole House Cooling Fan

Switch control _____ ; Noise level _____ . Gen. app. _____ . NOTES: _____

_____

FIREPLACE

Original _____ ; Steel insert _____ ; Damper operable _____ ; Glass doors _____ ; Spark screen _____ ; Gas logs _____ ; W/shut-off _____ ; Mortar condition _____ ; Hearth _____ . Gen. app. _____ . NOTES: _____

RECOMMENDED: _____

STAIRWAY

Size : _____ in. wide; Number of treads _____ . **Steps: Wood** _____ ; Steel _____ ; Concrete _____ . **Covered with:** Carpet _____ ; Tile _____ ; Lino. _____ ; Runner _____ ; Stain _____ ; Paint _____ . **Handrail:** 1-side _____ ; 2-sides _____ ; None _____ ; Anchored securely _____ . **Lighted:** Top _____ ; Bottom _____ . **Switch:** Single pole _____ ; 2-way _____ ; Too steep _____ ; Low headroom _____ . NOTES: _____

RECOMMENDED: _____

STAIRWAY ELEVATOR

Brand _____ ; Date last serviced _____ ; By: _____ ; Operable _____ . NOTES: _____
_____

SECURITY

Smoke Detector

Electric _____ ; Number operable _____ ; Battery _____ ; Number operable _____ .
NOTES: _____

Heat Detector

Electric _____ ; Number operable _____ ; Battery _____ ; Number operable _____ .
NOTES: _____

Burglar Alarm

Brand _____ ; Operable _____ ; Serviced by: _____ . NOTES: _____
_____

Dead-bolt Locks

Single _____ ; Number operable _____ ; Double _____ ; Number operable _____ ; Strike plates' condition _____ . NOTES: _____
_____

Intercom System

Brand _____ ; Number of stations _____ ; Number non-operable _____ ; Stations at entrance doors _____ . NOTES: _____
_____

N.B. If you have one or more electric smoke detectors in your home, you may qualify for a lower classification on your homeowner's insurance policy. Check with your insurance agent. This also applies to dead-bolt locks and burglar alarms.

PATIO DOOR

Number _____ ; Alum. _____ ; Wood _____ ; Sliding _____ ; Hinged _____ ; Paint _____ ;
Stain _____ ; Screen _____ ; Ease of operation _____ ; Lock securely _____ . Gen. app.
_____ . NOTES: _____
_____

CENTRAL VACUUM SYSTEM

Brand _____ . **Collection and motor assembly located in:** Basement _____ ; Garage _____ ;
Utility room _____ ; Other _____ . Number of outlets _____ . NOTES: _____
_____

SKYLIGHT

Brand _____ ; Number _____ ; Stationary _____ ; Vented _____ ; Manual _____ ; Elec.
_____ . NOTES: _____
_____

ATTIC

Access

Easy _____ ; Disappearing stairs _____ ; Crawl through door _____ ; Scuttle hole _____ .
Location: Garage _____ ; Hall _____ ; Closet _____ ; Other _____ . NOTES: _____
_____

Floored

Partial _____ ; Most _____ ; Little _____ ; None _____ ; Lighted _____ ; W/switch _____ ;
Pull chain _____ . NOTES: _____
_____

Insulation

Batt _____ ; Roll _____ ; Poured _____ ; Blown _____ ; To a depth of _____ in.
NOTES: _____

Dormer Walls

Insulated _____ . NOTES: _____
_____

Gable-end Louvers

Screen protector cover _____ . Gen. app. _____ . NOTES: _____
_____

Roof Ventilator

Number _____ . Control: Thermostat _____ ; Switch _____ . Operable _____ .
NOTES: _____

Watermarks

Roof decking _____ (New _____ Old _____); Rafters _____ (New _____ Old _____);
Insulation _____ (New _____ Old _____); Ceiling joists _____ (New _____ Old _____);
Ceiling _____ (New _____ Old _____); Chimney _____ (new _____ Old _____); Vents
_____ (New _____ Old _____). NOTES: _____
_____

Sufficient Head Room

NOTES: _____
_____

RECOMMENDED: _____
_____

SECTION SIX

GARAGE

Size

Ft./in. x _____ Ft./In. Attached _____ . Gen. app. _____ . NOTES: _____
_____
_____

Service Door

Wood _____; Steel _____; Painted _____; Stained _____; Operable _____; Locks securely
_____; In bind anywhere _____; Glass _____; Broken _____ . NOTES: _____
_____

Car Door

Number _____; Double _____; Single _____; Overhead _____; Sectional _____; 1-piece
_____; Sliding _____; Hinged _____; Wood _____; Steel _____; Fiberglass _____; Paint
_____; Stain _____ . **Condition of:** Hardware _____; Lock _____; Door _____ .
NOTES: _____
_____

Electronic Opener

Brand _____; Operable _____ . NOTES: _____
_____

Floor

Dirt _____; Concrete _____; Gravel _____ . Gen. app. _____ . NOTES: _____
_____

Walls

Plaster _____; Sheetrock _____; Paneling _____; Concrete block _____; Paint _____;
Other _____ . Gen. app. _____ . NOTES: _____
_____

Ceiling

Plaster _____; Sheetrock _____; Tile _____; Suspended _____; Staple _____; Paint
_____; Exposed rafters _____ . Gen. app. _____ . NOTES: _____
_____

Lights

Incandescent _____; Fluorescent _____; Ceiling _____; Wall _____; Swag _____; Other
_____; W/wall switch _____; Single pole _____; 2-way _____ . NOTES: _____
_____

Electric Receptacles

Number _____; Grounding type _____; Any switch-operated _____ . NOTES: _____
_____

Windows

(Mark number of each). Double-hung _____ ; Awn. _____ ; Casement _____ ; Slider _____ ;
Jalousie _____ ; Wood _____ ; Alum. _____ ; Steel _____ ; Vinyl _____ ; Lock _____ ;
Operable _____ ; Paint _____ ; Stain _____ ; Sill _____ ; Stool _____ ; Casing _____ .
Glazing: Single _____ ; Double _____ ; Triple _____ . Gen. app. _____ . NOTES: _____

RECOMMENDED: _____

Window Treatment

W/real estate _____ ; Drapes _____ ; Shutters _____ ; Blinds _____ ; Venetians _____ ;
Valance _____ . Gen. app. _____ . NOTES: _____

Roofing

Matches house roofing _____ . Gen. app. _____ . NOTES: _____

Siding

Matches house siding _____ . Gen. app. _____ . NOTES: _____

Gutters

Alum. _____ ; Steel _____ ; Plastic _____ ; O.G. _____ ; ½ round _____ ; Paint _____ ;
Joints & seams _____ ; Sufficient hangers _____ . Gen. app. _____ . NOTES: _____

Downspouts

Alum. _____ Steel _____ ; Plastic _____ ; Paint _____ ; Tied-in to sewer _____ ; **Empty onto:**
Ground _____ ; Splash blocks _____ . Gen. app. _____ . NOTES on guttering and downspouts:

RECOMMENDED: _____

CARPORT

Size

_____ x _____ ; Attached _____ ; Gen. app. _____ ; Freestanding _____ . **Made of:** Wood
_____ ; Alum. _____ ; Fiberglass _____ ; Other _____ . NOTES: _____

Roofing

Matches house roofing _____ . Gen. app. _____ . NOTES: _____

Gutters

Alum. _____ ; Steel _____ ; Plastic _____ ; O.G. _____ ; ½-round _____ ; Paint _____ ;
Joints and seams _____ ; Sufficient hangers _____ . Gen. app. _____ . NOTES: _____

Downspouts

Alum. _____ ; Steel _____ ; Plastic _____ ; Paint _____ ; Tied-in to sewer _____ . **Empty** onto: Ground _____ ; Splash blocks _____ . Gen. app. _____ . NOTES: _____

Supports

Wood _____ ; Steel _____ ; Alum. _____ ; Paint _____ . Gen. app. _____ . NOTES: _____

Lighting

Incandescent _____ ; Fluorescent _____ ; Other _____ . **Controlled w/switch:** Single pole _____ ; 2-way _____ . NOTES: _____

Electric Receptacles

Number _____ ; Grounding type _____ ; Cover _____ . NOTES: _____

NOTES on entire carport: _____
RECOMMENDED: _____

BREEZEWAY _____ ; SOLARIUM _____

Size

_____ x _____ . **Made of:** Wood _____ ; Alum. _____ . Enclosed: _____ ; Open _____ . NOTES: _____

ANY EVIDENCE OF MOISTURE PROBLEM _____ ; Recent _____ ; Old _____ . NOTES: _____

Floor

Concrete _____ ; Wood _____ ; Paint _____ ; Lino. _____ ; Slate _____ ; Ceramic _____ ; Tile _____ ; Carpet _____ ; Other _____ . Gen. app. _____ . NOTES: _____

Ceiling

Plaster _____ ; Sheetrock _____ ; Alum. _____ ; Tile _____ ; Wood _____ ; Paint _____ ; Stain _____ . Gen. app. _____ . NOTES: _____

Walls

Plaster _____ ; Sheetrock _____ ; Paneling _____ Paint _____ ; Stain _____ ; Other _____ . Gen. app. _____ . NOTES: _____

Windows

(Mark number of each). Double-hung _____ ; Awn. _____ ; Casement _____ ; Slider _____ ;
Jalousie _____ ; Wood _____ ; Alum. _____ ; Steel _____ ; Vinyl _____ ; Lock _____ ;
Operable _____ ; Paint _____ ; Stain _____ ; Sill _____ ; Stool _____ ; Casing _____ .
Glazing: Single _____ ; Double _____ ; Triple _____ . Gen. app. _____ . NOTES: _____

RECOMMENDED: _____

Window Treatment

W/real estate _____ ; Drapes _____ ; Shutters _____ ; Blinds _____ ; Venetians _____ ;
Valance _____ . Gen. app. _____ . NOTES: _____

Ceiling Fan

W/real estate _____ ; W/lights _____ ; Operable _____ ; Sep. wall control _____ . Gen. app.
_____ . NOTES: _____

Built-ins

(Identify and comment) _____

_____

_____

_____

_____

_____

Heating

Separate _____ ; Gas _____ ; W/shut-off _____ ; Electric _____ ; From house unit _____ ;
None _____ . NOTES: _____

Cooling

Separate _____ ; Window A/C _____ ; From house unit _____ ; None _____ .
NOTES: _____

Doors

Into house _____ ; Into garage _____ ; Separate entrance _____ . Gen. app. _____ .
NOTES: _____

Electric Receptacles

Number _____ ; Grounding type _____ . NOTES: _____

Roofing

Match house roofing _____ . Gen. app. _____ . NOTES: _____

Gutters

Alum. _____ ; Steel _____ ; Plastic _____ ; O.G. _____ ; ½-round _____ ; Paint _____ ;
Joints and seams _____ ; Sufficient hangers _____ . Gen. app. _____ . NOTES: _____

Downspouts

Alum. _____ ; Steel _____ ; Plastic _____ ; Paint _____ ; Tied-in to sewer _____ . **Empty**
onto: Ground _____ ; Splash blocks _____ . NOTES: _____

RECOMMENDED: _____

PORCH

Size

_____ x _____ . **Made of:** Wood _____ ; Alum. _____ . Enclosed _____ ; Open _____ .
NOTES: _____

ANY EVIDENCE OF MOISTURE PROBLEM _____ ; Recent _____ ; Old _____ .
NOTES: _____

Floor

Concrete _____ ; Wood _____ ; Paint _____ ; Lino. _____ ; Slate _____ ; Ceramic _____ ;
Tile _____ ; Carpet _____ ; Other _____ . Gen. app. _____ . NOTES: _____

Ceiling

Plaster _____ ; Sheetrock _____ ; Alum. _____ ; Tile _____ ; Wood _____ ; Paint _____ ;
Stain _____ . Gen. app. _____ . NOTES: _____

Walls

Plaster _____ ; Sheetrock _____ ; Paneling _____ ; Paint _____ ; Stain _____ ; Other _____ .
Gen. app. _____ . NOTES: _____

Windows

(Mark number of each). Double-hung _____ ; Awn. _____ ; Casement _____ ; Slider _____ ;
Jalousie _____ ; Wood _____ ; Alum. _____ ; Steel _____ ; Vinyl _____ ; Lock _____ ;
Operable _____ ; Paint _____ ; Stain _____ ; Sill _____ ; Stool _____ ; Casing _____ .
Glazing: Single _____ ; Double _____ ; Triple _____ . Gen. app. _____ . NOTES: _____

RECOMMENDED: _____

Window Treatment

W/real estate _____ ; Drapes _____ ; Shutters _____ ; Blinds _____ ; Venetians _____ ;
Valance _____ . Gen. app. _____ . NOTES: _____

Ceiling Fan
W/real estate _____ ; W/lights _____ ; Operable _____ ; Sep. wall control _____ . Gen. app. _____ . NOTES: _____
_____

Built-ins
(Identify and comment) _____
_____
_____
_____

Heating
Separate _____ ; Gas _____ ; W/shut-off _____ ; Electric _____ ; From house unit _____ ;
None _____ . NOTES: _____
_____

Cooling
Separate _____ ; Window A/C _____ ; From house unit _____ ; None _____ .
NOTES: _____
_____

Doors
Into house _____ ; Into garage _____ ; Separate entrance _____ . Gen. app. _____ .
NOTES: _____
_____

Electric Receptacles
Number _____ ; Grounding type _____ . NOTES: _____
_____

Roofing
Matches house roofing _____ . Gen. app. _____ . NOTES: _____
_____

Gutters
Alum. _____ ; Steel _____ ; Plastic _____ ; O.G. _____ ; ½-round _____ ; Paint _____ ;
Joints and seams _____ ; Sufficient hangers _____ . Gen. app. _____ . NOTES: _____
_____

Downspouts
Alum. _____ ; Steel _____ ; Plastic _____ ; Paint _____ ; Tied-in to sewer _____ . **Empty**
onto: Ground _____ ; Splash blocks _____ . NOTES: _____
_____

RECOMMENDED: _____

SECOND PORCH

Size

_____ x _____ . **Made of:** Wood _____ ; Alum. _____ ; Enclosed _____ ; Open _____ .
NOTES: _____
_____

ANY EVIDENCE OF MOISTURE PROBLEM _____ ; Recent _____ ; Old _____ .
NOTES: _____
_____
_____
_____

Floor

Concrete _____ ; Wood _____ ; Paint _____ ; Lino. _____ ; Slate _____ ; Ceramic _____ ;
Tile _____ ; Carpet _____ ; Other _____ . Gen. app. _____ . NOTES: _____
_____

Ceiling

Plaster _____ ; Sheetrock _____ ; Alum. _____ ; Tile _____ ; Wood _____ ; Paint _____ ;
Stain _____ . Gen. app. _____ . NOTES: _____
_____

Walls

Plaster _____ ; Sheetrock _____ ; Paneling _____ ; Paint _____ ; Stain _____ ; Other _____ .
Gen. app. _____ . NOTES: _____
_____

Windows

(Mark number of each). Double-hung _____ ; Awn. _____ ; Casement _____ ; Slider _____ ;
Jalousie _____ ; Wood _____ ; Alum. _____ ; Steel _____ ; Vinyl _____ ; Lock _____ ;
Operable _____ ; Paint _____ ; Stain _____ ; Sill _____ ; Stool _____ ; Casing _____ .
Glazing: Single _____ ; Double _____ ; Triple _____ . Gen. app. _____ . NOTES: _____

RECOMMENDED: _____

Window Treatment

W/real estate _____ ; Drapes _____ ; Shutters _____ ; Blinds _____ ; Venetians _____ ;
Valance _____ . Gen. app. _____ . NOTES: _____
_____

Ceiling Fan

W/real estate _____ ; W/lights _____ ; Operable _____ ; Sep. wall control _____ . Gen. app.
_____ . NOTES: _____
_____

Built-ins

(Identify and comment) _____
_____
_____
_____

Heating

Separate _____ ; Gas _____ ; W/shut-off _____ ; Electric _____ ; From house unit _____ ;
None _____ . NOTES: _____
_____

Cooling

Separate _____ ; Window A/C _____ ; From house unit _____ ; None _____ .
NOTES: _____
_____

Doors

Into house _____ ; Into garage _____ ; Separate entrance _____ . Gen. app. _____ .
NOTES: _____
_____

Electric Receptacles

Number _____ ; Grounding type _____ . NOTES: _____
_____

Roofing

Matches house roofing _____ . Gen. app. _____ . NOTES: _____
_____

Gutters

Alum. _____ ; Steel _____ ; Plastic _____ ; O.G. _____ ; ½-round _____ ; Paint _____ ;
Joints and seams _____ ; Sufficient hangers _____ . Gen. app. _____ . NOTES: _____
_____

Downspouts

Alum. _____ ; Steel _____ ; Plastic _____ ; Paint _____ ; Tied-in to sewer _____ . **Empty**
onto: Ground _____ ; Splash blocks _____ . NOTES: _____
_____
RECOMMENDED: _____

OUTBUILDING

Size

_____ x _____ . **Made of:** Wood _____ ; Alum. _____ ; Enclosed _____ ; Open _____ .
NOTES: _____
ANY EVIDENCE OF MOISTURE PROBLEM _____ ; Recent _____ ; Old _____ .
NOTES: _____
_____

Floor

Concrete _____ ; wood _____ ; Paint _____ ; Lino. _____ ; Slate _____ ; Ceramic _____ ;
Tile _____ ; Carpet _____ ; Other _____ . Gen. app. _____ . NOTES: _____
_____

Ceiling

Plastic _____ ; Sheetrock _____ ; Alum. _____ ; Tile _____ ; Wood _____ ; Paint _____ ;
Stain _____ . Gen. app. _____ . NOTES: _____
_____

Walls

Plaster _____ ; Sheetrock _____ ; Paneling _____ ; Paint _____ ; Stain _____ ; Other _____ .
Gen. app. _____ . NOTES: _____
_____

Windows

(Mark number of each). Double-hung _____ ; Awn. _____ ; Casement _____ ; Slider _____ ;
Jalousie _____ ; Wood _____ ; Alum. _____ ; Steel _____ ; Vinyl _____ ; Lock _____ ;
Operable _____ ; Paint _____ ; Stain _____ ; Sill _____ ; Stool _____ ; Casing _____ .
Glazing: Single _____ ; Double _____ ; Triple _____ . Gen. app. _____ . NOTES: _____
_____

RECOMMENDED: _____

Window Treatment

W/real estate _____ ; Drapes _____ ; Shutters _____ ; Blinds _____ ; Venetians _____ ;
Valance _____ . Gen. app. _____ . NOTES: _____
_____

Ceiling Fan

W/real estate _____ ; W/lights _____ ; Operable _____ ; Sep. wall control _____ . Gen. app.
_____ . NOTES: _____
_____

Built-ins

(Identify and comment) _____
_____
_____
_____

Heating

Separate _____ ; Gas _____ ; W/shut-off _____ ; Electric _____ ; From house unit _____ ;
None _____ . NOTES: _____
_____

Cooling

Separate _____ ; Window A/C _____ ; From house unit _____ ; None _____ .
NOTES: _____

Doors

Into house _____ ; Into garage _____ ; Separate entrance _____ . Gen. app. _____ .
NOTES: _____

Electric Receptacles

Number _____ ; Grounding type _____ . NOTES: _____
_____

Roofing

Matches house roofing _____ . Gen. app. _____ . NOTES: _____

_____

Gutters

Alum. _____ ; Steel _____ ; Plastic _____ ; O.G. _____ ; ½-round _____ ; Paint _____ ;
Joints and seams _____ ; Sufficient hangers _____ . Gen. app. _____ . NOTES: _____

_____

Downspouts

Alum. _____ ; Steel _____ ; Plastic _____ ; Paint _____ ; Tied-in to sewer _____ . **Empty**
onto: Ground _____ ; Splash blocks _____ . NOTES: _____

_____

RECOMMENDED: _____

SECTION SEVEN

FRONT ENTRANCE

Size _____ in. x _____ in.; Wood _____ ; Steel _____ . **Casing:** Inside _____ ; Outside _____ . Paint _____ ; Stain _____ ; Other _____ ; Operable _____ ; Bind anywhere _____ ; Close securely _____ . Gen. app. _____ . NOTES: _____
_____

Lock

Key-in-knob _____ . **Deadbolt:** _____ ; Double _____ ; Single _____ ; Other _____ .
NOTES: _____

Weatherstripping

Part of frame _____ ; Jamb-up _____ ; Alum. _____ ; Wood _____ ; Copper strip _____ .
Gen. app. _____ . NOTES: _____
_____

Special Features of Door

_____
_____

Privacy Viewer

_____
_____

Storm Door

Alum. _____ ; Wood _____ ; Operable _____ . Lock _____ ; Operable _____ .
NOTES: _____

Doorbell

Operable _____ . Chimes _____ ; Operable _____ . NOTES: _____
_____

RECOMMENDED: _____
_____

SIDE ENTRANCE

Size _____ in. x _____ in.; Wood _____ ; Steel _____ . **Frame:** _____ . **Casing:** Inside _____ ; Outside _____ . Paint _____ ; Stain _____ ; Other _____ ; Operable _____ ; Bind anywhere _____ ; Close securely _____ . Gen. app. _____ . NOTES: _____
_____

Lock

Key-in-knob _____ . **Deadbolt:** _____ ; Double _____ ; Single _____ ; Other _____ .
NOTES: _____

Weatherstripping

Part of frame _____ ; Jamb-up _____ ; Alum. _____ ; Wood _____ ; Copper strip _____ .
Gen. app. _____ . NOTES: _____
_____

Special Features of Door

_____
_____

Privacy Viewer

_____
_____

Storm Door

Alum. _____ ; Wood _____ ; Operable _____ . Lock _____ ; Operable _____ .
NOTES: _____
_____
_____

Doorbell

Operable _____ . Chimes _____ ; Operable _____ . NOTES: _____
_____
RECOMMENDED: _____

REAR ENTRANCE

Size _____ in. x _____ in.; Wood _____ ; Steel _____ . **Frame:** _____ . **Casing:** Inside
_____ ; Outside _____ . Paint _____ ; Stain _____ ; Other _____ ; Operable _____ ; Bind
anywhere _____ ; Close securely _____ . Gen. app. _____ . NOTES: _____
_____

Lock

Key-in-knob _____ . **Deadbolt:** _____ ; Double _____ ; Single _____ ; Other _____ .
NOTES: _____

Weatherstripping

Part of frame _____ ; Jamb-up _____ ; Alum. _____ ; Wood _____ ; Copper strip _____ .
Gen. app. _____ . NOTES: _____
_____

Special Features of Door

_____
_____

Privacy Viewer

_____
_____

Storm Door

Alum. _____ ; Wood _____ ; Operable _____ . Lock _____ ; Operable _____ .
NOTES: _____
_____

Doorbell

Operable _____ . Chimes _____ ; Operable _____ . NOTES: _____
_____

RECOMMENDED: _____

WINDOWS
(from the outside)

Jalousie _____ ; Hopper _____ ; Cottage _____ ; Oriel _____ ; Stationary _____ ; Wood
_____ ; Alum. _____ ; Steel _____ ; Vinyl _____ ; Lock _____ ; Operable _____ ; Paint
_____ ; Stain _____ ; Sill _____ ; Stool _____ ; Casing _____ . **Glazing: Single** _____ ;
Double _____ ; Triple _____ . Gen. app. _____ . NOTES: _____
_____

RECOMMENDED: _____

Storm Windows

Wood _____ ; Alum. _____ ; W/screens _____ ; Broken glass _____ ; Broken sash _____ ;
Broken frames _____ . NOTES: _____
_____

Caulking

NOTES: _____
OTHER WINDOWS NOT NOTED BEFORE OR ABOVE: _____
_____

RECOMMENDED: _____

SILL COCK

Number _____ ; Frost-free _____ ; Dripping _____ (Be certain to test each if weather permits).
NOTES: _____
RECOMMENDED: _____

SECOND-STORY OUTSIDE STAIRS

Size _____ in. W x Number of treads _____ ; Wood _____ ; Steel _____ ; Concrete _____ ;
Covered _____ ; Enclosed _____ . **Handrail** _____ ; 1-side _____ ; 2-sides _____ ; None
_____ ; Anchored securely _____ ; Enclosed _____ ; Open _____ ; Landing _____ ;
Protective rail _____ ; Secure _____ ; Lighted: _____ ; Controlled w/switch: _____ ; Single
pole _____ ; 2-way _____ . NOTES: _____
_____

RECOMMENDED: _____

SECTION EIGHT

AWNINGS

Number

Wood _____ ; Alum. _____ ; Steel _____ ; Fabric _____ ; Painted _____ ; Secure to wall _____ . Gen. app. _____ . NOTES: _____

RECOMMENDED: _____

ROOF

General Appearance

Age _____ yrs.; Original roof _____ ; Second roof _____ ; Third roof _____ ; Gable _____ ; Hip _____ ; Gambrel _____ ; Mansard _____ ; A-frame _____ ; Flat _____ ; Steep _____ ; Low-pitch _____ . **Covered with:** 3-in-1 Tab _____ ; Asphalt composition _____ ; Fiberglass composition _____ ; Lock-tab _____ ; Slate _____ ; Wood shingles _____ ; Metal _____ ; Alum. _____ ; Built-up _____ ; Other _____ . NOTES: _____

Roof Edging

Steel _____ ; Alum. _____ ; Plastic _____ ; Perimeter of roof _____ . NOTES: _____
_____

Dormer

Number _____ . Gen. app. _____ . NOTES: _____

Chimney

Brick _____ ; Concrete block _____ ; Metal _____ ; Rain protector _____ ; Bird protector _____ . NOTES: _____

Roof TV Antenna

Attached securely _____ . NOTES: _____

NOTES GENERALLY ON ENTIRE ROOF: _____
_____
_____
_____

RECOMMENDED: _____

GUTTERING AND DOWNSPOUTS

Guttering

Steel _____ ; Alum. _____ ; Plastic _____ ; Paint _____ ; O.G. _____ ; ½-round _____ ;
Anchored securely _____ ; Drainage pitch _____ ; Seams and joints _____ ; Holes _____ ;
Loose hangers _____ ; Gutter guard _____ . Gen. app. _____ . NOTES: _____

RECOMMENDED: _____

Downspouts

Steel _____ ; Alum. _____ ; Plastic _____ ; Paint _____ ; Anchored securely _____ ; Tied-in
to sewer _____ ; Empty onto splash block _____ ; Away from house _____ . NOTES: _____

RECOMMENDED: _____

FASCIA

Wood _____ ; Painted _____ ; Covered w/: Alum. _____ ; Plastic _____ . Gen. app. _____ .
NOTES: _____
RECOMMENDED: _____

SOFFIT

Protrusion from house: _____ in.; Rafters exposed _____ ; Painted _____ ; Covered with alum.
_____ ; Vents _____ ; Qty. _____ ; Size _____ . Gen. app. _____ . NOTES: _____

RECOMMENDED: _____

SIDING

Brick _____ ; Concrete block _____ ; Glazed tile _____ ; Stone _____ ; Wood _____ ; Alum.
_____ ; Vinyl _____ ; Steel _____ ; Stucco _____ ; Soft (brick-stone) _____ ; Asbestos
_____ ; Fiberglass imitation stone _____ ; Painted _____ ; Stained _____ . Gen. app. _____ .
NOTES: _____
RECOMMENDED: _____

Electric Receptacles

Number _____ ; Grounding type _____ ; Protective covers _____ . NOTES: _____

OUTDOOR LIGHTING

(Test and mark each with kind of switch controlling it): **T** = Timer; **P** = Photo; **S** = Single pole; and
"2" = 2-Way)

Location

Porch _____ ; Ceiling _____ ; Wall _____ ; Soffit _____ . Gable: _____ . Garage: _____ .
Yard: _____ ; Front _____ ; Side _____ ; Rear _____ ; Dusk-to-dawn _____ .
NOTES: _____
RECOMMENDED: _____

SEPTIC SYSTEM

Date last cleaned: _____ ; By: _____ ; Sunken area in field bed _____ ; Strong odor in field bed area _____ ; Septic tank lid cracked _____ . NOTES: _____

RECOMMENDED: _____

LANDSCAPE

General appearance: _____ ; Grass _____ ; Shrubs _____ ; Flowers _____ ; Trees _____ ;
Limbs need to be _____ ; Have been _____ ; Trimmed.

Garden: _____ ; Flower _____ ; Vegetable _____ . NOTES: _____
Contour of lot for drainage: North _____ ; _____ East _____ ; _____ West _____ ;
South _____ ; _____ . NOTES: _____

FENCING

General appearance: _____ ; Wood _____ ; Steel _____ ; Brick _____ ; Concrete block
_____ ; Other _____ . NOTES: _____

Type: Chain-link _____ ; Stockade _____ ; Split-rail _____ ; Other _____ .
Gate: Operable _____ . NOTES: _____

RECOMMENDED: _____

DRIVEWAY

General appearance: _____ ; Concrete _____ ; Chat _____ ; Asphalt _____ ; Brick _____ ;
Dirt _____ ; Other _____ . Serious upheaval in paving materials _____ . NOTES: _____

RECOMMENDED: _____

WALKS

General appearance: _____ ; Concrete _____ ; Chat _____ ; Asphalt _____ ; Brick _____ ;
Dirt _____ ; Other _____ . Serious upheaval in paving materials _____ . NOTES: _____

RECOMMENDED: _____

WOOD PATIO

General appearance: _____ ; Age: _____ yrs. **Type of wood:** Pine _____ ; Cedar _____ ;
Redwood _____ ; Other _____ . Pressure-treated _____ ; Painted _____ ; Stained _____ ;
Sturdy _____ . Handrails _____ ; Seats _____ ; Built-ins _____ . NOTES: _____

RECOMMENDED: _____

GAS GRILL

W/real estate: _____ ; Age: _____ yrs.; Brand _____ ; Gas: L.P. _____ ; Natural _____ ;
Operable _____ . NOTES: _____
_____

SWIMMING POOL

General appearance: _____ ; Age: _____ yrs.; In-ground _____ ; Above ground _____ ; Steel
_____ ; Alum. _____ ; Fiberglass _____ . **Depth:** At shallow end _____ ; At deep end _____ .
Circular _____ ; Rectangular _____ ; Other _____ .

Apron

Concrete _____ ; Wood _____ ; Other _____ .

Cover for Pool

NOTES: _____
RECOMMENDED: _____

HOT TUB

General appearance: _____ ; Age: _____ yrs.; Brand _____ . **Located in:** House _____ ;
Garage _____ ; Yard _____ . Connected to separate circuit _____ ; Ground-fault type _____ .
NOTES: _____

SAUNA

General appearance: _____ ; Age: _____ yrs.; Brand _____ . **Located in:** House _____ ;
Garage _____ ; Yard _____ . Connected to separate circuit _____ ; Ground-fault type _____ .
NOTES: _____

OUTDOOR FURNITURE/PLAY EQUIPMENT

W/real estate _____ ; Steel _____ ; Wood _____ ; Alum. _____ ; Plastic _____ ; Concrete
_____ ; Paint _____ . NOTES: _____
_____

PUBLIC WALKS, CURBS AND GUTTERS

General appearance: _____ . NOTES: _____
_____
RECOMMENDED: _____

ALLEY

General appearance: _____ . NOTES: _____
_____
RECOMMENDED: _____

OTHER ITEMS

Recap of items in serious need of special attention:

_____
_____
_____
_____
_____
_____
_____
_____
_____
_____
_____
_____
_____
_____
_____
_____
_____

General observation of the entire house and grounds displays the pride of ownership to be:

EXCEPTIONAL [   ]
AVERAGE [   ]
MARGINAL [   ]
BELOW AVERAGE [   ]

This checklist has been provided in order to assist you in your search for defects in the house you are purchasing or selling. Hopefully it has helped you.

GOOD LUCK!